THE LITTLE GUIDES

BIRDS

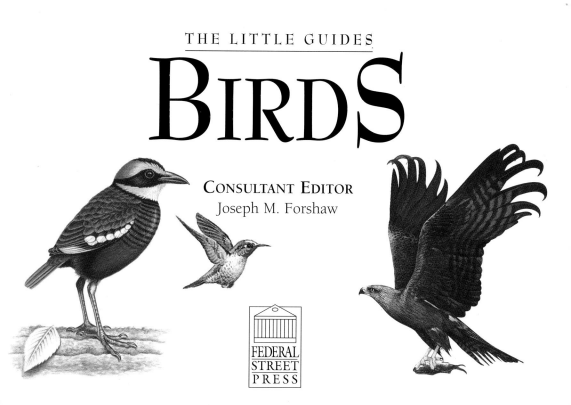

THE LITTLE GUIDES

BIRDS

CONSULTANT EDITOR
Joseph M. Forshaw

FEDERAL
STREET
PRESS

Copyright © 2000 Weldon Owen Pty Ltd

Federal Street Press is a trademark of Federal Street Press,
a division of Merriam-Webster, Incorporated.

This 2001 edition published by
Federal Street Press
A Division of Merriam-Webster, Incorporated
PO Box 281
Springfield, MA 01102

Federal Street Press books are available for bulk purchase
for sales promotion and premium use. For deatils write the
manager of special sales, Federal Street Press, PO Box 281,
Springfield, MA 01102

Publisher: Sheena Coupe
Managing Editor: Helen Bateman
Senior Designer: Kylie Mulquin
Editorial Coordinator: Tracey Gibson
Production Manager: Helen Creeke
Production Assistant: Kylie Lawson
Business Manager: Emily Jahn
Vice President International Sales: Stuart Laurence

Project Editor: John Mapps
Designer: Avril Makula
Consultant Editor: Joseph M. Forshaw

ISBN 1-892859-21-1

Color reproduction by Colourscan Co Pte Ltd
Printed by LeeFung-Asco Printers
Printed in China

01 02 03 04 05   5 4 3 2 1

CONTENTS

PART ONE

THE WORLD OF BIRDS

PART TWO
KINDS OF BIRDS

THE WORLD OF BIRDS

UNDERSTANDING BIRDS

The spectacular diversity of birds is a delight—their shapes, their plumage, their songs and their power of flight have been a source of fascination for centuries. But there is much more to birds, of course, than these outward signs. Just how much more is detailed in this chapter, which uncovers the many important physical aspects of a bird's life: its complex, made-for-flight anatomy; the relationship between lifestyle and wing type; the ingenious engineering of the feather; the reasons for the almost endless array of plumage variations; and the innumerable ways in which species fill niches in almost all habitats, from the polar wastes to the tropics, and from the oceans to the deserts.

INTRODUCING BIRDS

Well over 9,000 species of birds inhabit the world today. The power of flight makes them among the most mobile of all animals. There are other animals that roam widely, but birds alone can, at least in principle, go anywhere they please on the Earth's surface.

The avian world Although most numerous in marshes, woodlands and rain forests, birds inhabit the most inhospitable of deserts, and have been seen within a few miles of both poles. Some never stray from home in their entire lives, but others can, and frequently do, span entire oceans or continents, sometimes in a single flight.

Birds—great and small There are about 9,300 species of birds in the world, and they range from the bee humming-bird, which weighs little more than a dime, to the imposing ostrich, which stands taller than a man and weighs over 300 pounds (136 kg).

SPECIES DIVERSITY
The map shows how species density varies in different regions. Tropical rain forests have most species, polar icecaps fewest. Most temperate areas have similar numbers of species.

☐ 50 or fewer species
☐ 50 to 250 species
☐ 250 to 500 species
☐ 500 to 1,000 species
☐ 1,000 to 1,500 species

12

A GIANT AMONG BIRDS

A male ostrich may weigh as much as 300 pounds (136 kg) and stand 9 feet (2.75 m) tall. The extinct elephant-bird of Malagasy was even larger: This truly enormous bird was over 10 feet (3 m) tall and is estimated to have weighed 1,000 pounds (450 kg); its eggs contained about 2 gallons (9 L) of liquid.

Among these species can be found almost any color of the rainbow. These colors may be arranged in the dazzling patterns found in breeding peacocks or in the astonishingly effective camouflage of birds such as the tawny frogmouth, which evades predators by imitating a dead tree stump.

Athletes of inner space

Golden-plovers, taking off with a load of fuel almost equal to their own weight, fly nonstop from Alaska to Hawaii and back each year, while peregrine falcons reach speeds approaching 200 miles (320 km) per hour as they dive upon their winged prey. In contrast to these masters of the air, there are a few birds—ostriches, emus and rheas, for example—that cannot fly at all.

TINY FLIER

Most hummingbirds are small, but Anna's hummingbird, of southwestern North America, is tiny. It measures 4 inches (10 cm) in length and weighs just a few ounces.

THE ORIGINS OF BIRDS

The patchy fossil record means that the exact origins of birds are still uncertain, but it has long been thought that they evolved from reptiles. The earliest known bird, *Archaeopteryx*, lived about 150 million years ago.

REPTILE-BIRD
An artist's conception of *Archaeopteryx* gives some idea of the animal's mixture of reptilian and avian characteristics: It has teeth, tiny claws on the forewing, and feathers.

Fossil evidence Birds are not well represented in fossil deposits for several reasons, one being that bird bones are particularly easily fragmented. Another reason is that few landbirds die where their remains can be buried in waterlaid sediments, the richest source of fossils. It has been estimated that between the time of *Archaeopteryx* and the present day, between 1.5 million and 2 million bird species have existed. Of these, we have evidence for the existence of fewer than 12,000 species!

"Feathered dinosaurs"
One theory of bird origins links birds to a specific subgroup of dinosaurs called theropods, which were common 200 million years ago. An important piece of evidence for this link is a U-shaped furcula or "wishbone" found both in birds and in some theropods. In birds, this feature plays an important role in flight. In the dinosaurs it probably evolved as a support for the short forelimbs that they used for catching prey.

The first bird The fossilized bird known as *Archaeopteryx* is the most important evidence of the link between birds and dinosaurs. It was certainly a bird, as it had feathers and a U-shaped "wishbone", but it also possessed definite reptilian characteristics, including teeth and clawed digits on the forewing. About the size of a crow, *Archaeopteryx* was a predator, and probably caught insects or small vertebrates, such as lizards. It lived about 150 million years ago. Scientists are unsure about its capacity for flight. Some claim that it would have been a weak flier, while others argue that it would have been capable of sustained flight.

Cretaceous birds Though only slightly more recent than *Archaeopteryx*, the birds of the early Cretaceous period (about 130 million years ago) were much more like modern birds.

TERATORNIS
Many fossils of this large, vulturelike predator that lived in western North America in the Pleistocene epoch have been found in the Rancho La Brea tar pits in California.

Most were strong fliers. Probably the most famous of the Cretaceous fossil birds are *Hesperornis* and *Ichthyornis* from North America. Both are notable in that they had teeth, a condition prominent in *Archaeopteryx* and its theropod ancestors. *Hesperornis* was a flightless, fish-eating, diving-bird, whereas *Ichthyornis* was a strong flier.

The Pleistocene epoch Fossils of the Pleistocene epoch (2 million to 10,000 years ago) include many species that are alive today, as well as numerous species that are now extinct. The Rancho La Brea tar pits in California have yielded specimens of species like *Teratornis*, which used its 12½-foot (3.8-m) wingspan to soar across the skies of North America.

Modern birds Present-day birds really are not so "modern," since most of the species we know today have been around for thousands of years. Indeed, there were probably about 11,500 species during the Pleistocene—about 1,500 more than exist today. The number of species probably reached a peak from 500,000 to 250,000 years ago, and has been in gradual decline ever since.

NAMING THE BIRDS

Taxonomy is the science of classifying living things. Early taxonomists based classifications of birds almost entirely on external appearances, but these days systems of classification have become much more sophisticated.

The species concept The keystone of modern taxonomy (and the focus of bird identification) is the classification of species. A species is defined as a population whose members do not freely interbreed with members of other populations (although this is sometimes difficult to establish one way or the other). Within a species, there are often groups or populations which differ in minor ways, such as in size or plumage coloration. These interbreeding groups are recognized as sub-species or races. Populations separated by geographical barriers (such as oceans) are also known as isolates.

Higher categories All birds are related to some extent, and taxonomy establishes the different levels of relationship. Above the species level, related species are grouped into genera, related genera into families, and related families into orders. Intermediate categories are used by taxonomists

SUBSPECIES
A subspecies is a distinct geographical population of a species. Two subspecies of the yellow wagtail are *Motacilla flava flavissima* (left), of Britain, and *M. f. flava* (above), of continental Europe.

to express finer distinctions. Together, birds form a class, Aves, and, along with other classes of backboned animals, this class is part of the subphylum Vertebrata (the vertebrates), and of the animal kingdom.

What's in a name? Most species have a common name (the English name in English-speaking countries) and a scientific name consisting of two main elements: the genus and the specific name. Where there are subspecies, the subspecies name is sometimes included as a third element. The scientific name is latinized and highlighted in a different type (normally italic). Only the generic name is capitalized.

Avoiding confusion The purpose of scientific names is to provide an internationally recognizable and consistent system of classification. The common name of a single species may vary between languages and countries, but its scientific name will always be the same. Conversely, one or more birds may be known by the same common name in different countries, but may not be related

at all. For example, we often talk about "robins" in America, but the "robins" of the United Kingdom and Australia are quite different birds. Use of the scientific name eliminates any confusion.

Taxonomy today Work in the field of biochemical research, especially analysis of DNA (deoxyribonucleic acid)— the essential genetic material—has proved a powerful tool in clarifying the relationships of birds. Advances in scientific procedures have led to new techniques being applied to determining alliances between kinds of bird. Taxonomy now draws on a synthesis of data from many fields of biology, including paleontology, ecology, physiology, behavior, and DNA and protein analysis.

CLASSIFYING THE REDSTART

The purposes of taxonomy are twofold: to assign a unique name to each species and to place it within a structure of relationships. The American redstart, for example, is classified in the following way:
- Class Aves
- Order Passeriformes
- Family Parulidae
- Genus *Setophaga*
- Species *ruticilla*

Subspecies may also be named.

BIRD ANATOMY

If you compare the skeleton, muscle and organ systems of a bird with those of a human, you will find many points of similarity. But there are, of course, enormous differences. Almost all of these differences are the result of profound modifications in birds to enable sustained flight.

Skeletal system The sternum, or breastbone, lies in the same relative position and serves the same basic function as the sternum in our own body. However, in birds it is much bigger in relative terms, and bears, projecting at right angles, the most obvious and distinctive of avian skeletal structures: a large flat keel (called the carina). This serves as a point of attachment for the huge pectoral muscles used to flap the wings. Another unique feature of the avian skeleton is that in many birds the collarbones have fused to form a rigid brace for the wings, called the furcula or "wishbone."

Breathing A bird's respiratory system is remarkably efficient. A multitude of empty spaces (called pulmonary sacs or air sacs) extend throughout the body, in many birds extending even into the hollow bones. Air flows through this system of interconnected sacs almost like blood in the circulatory system. The lungs are located so that air flows through them, not in and out as in other vertebrates. Oxygen transfer to the blood is thus a continuous process, taking place during both inhalation and exhalation. This system is so efficient that, paradoxically, birds get by with much smaller lungs than other vertebrates.

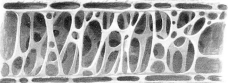

HOLLOW BONES
Many of the larger bones in a bird's skeleton are thin-walled and hollow to minimize weight, but braced and structured inside to maximize strength.

Sensory systems The sense of smell is generally less important to birds than their sight and hearing, which are acute. In experiments, birds were able to distinguish between sounds that are repeated so rapidly that to the human ear they become inextricably fused.

Sight Birds' eyes are among the most sophisticated sensory organs in the animal kingdom. The eye of a large eagle, for example, is about the same size as a human eye, but has many more sensory elements (rods and cones) in the retina (the rear inner surface of the eye on which the image is formed). A unique feature of birds' eyes is the pecten, a structure that emerges from the retina. It is believed to help improve the supply of oxygen and nutrients to the light-sensitive cells of the retina.

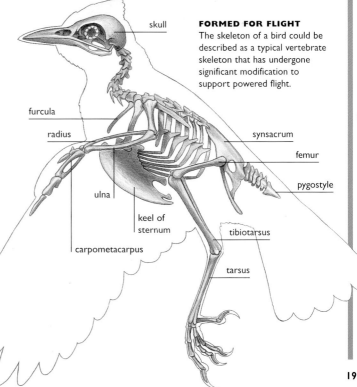

FORMED FOR FLIGHT
The skeleton of a bird could be described as a typical vertebrate skeleton that has undergone significant modification to support powered flight.

skull

furcula

radius

synsacrum

femur

pygostyle

ulna

keel of sternum

tibiotarsus

carpometacarpus

tarsus

FEATHERS AND PLUMAGE

One of the marvels of animal engineering, the feather is light, flexible and strong. Feathers play a critical part in controlling a bird's internal temperature, and an obviously crucial role in flight. As well, plumage colors and patterns are used in displays and for species recognition.

Material and design The material from which a feather is built is keratin, the same substance that makes up our hair and nails. Right along the length of the central stalk (rachis) of a feather, structures called barbs emerge in parallel and on one plane, in an arrangement reminiscent of a plastic comb. Each barb in turn carries even smaller structures called barbules, arranged in the same way along its length. The whole assembly is held together by myriad tiny hooks on the barbules which lock onto the barbules of the neighboring barb.

Preening A bird spends part of each day making minor repairs to tears in its feathers, an act called preening. Most repairs involve reattaching the hooks of the barbules, rather like reclosing Velcro strips. The bird does this by nibbling along the barbs of each feather to bring the "Velcro" in contact again.

sheath

rachis

barbs

HOW A FEATHER GROWS
A new feather starts out looking like a plastic drinking straw. Within this sheath, the feather itself develops, its barbs and barbules crammed in a tight spiral. The tip of the sheath splits, allowing the feather to unfold, fanlike, into its final shape.

TYPES OF FEATHERS
Most contour or body feathers (left) are small, blunt and fluffy, whereas flight feathers (below) are longer, stiffer and smoother.

Other feathers Other types of feathers include down feathers, which form a soft underlayer that further insulates the bird. Some birds, such as parrots, pigeons and herons, also have specialized feathers called powder-down. These break down into a waxy powder that the bird spreads throughout its plumage during preening.

Plumage The mass of feathers on a bird's body constitutes its plumage. In most birds, feathers tend to clump in distinct tracts, known as pterylae, and the intervening areas (the apterylae) are bare. Feathers come in a dazzling range of colors. Plumage coloration and pattern help birds to recognize other individuals of their own species and feature prominently in their displays.

Feather types Most feathers are either contour or flight feathers. Contour feathers cover the body, and are basically there to keep the bird warm. Flight feathers are those directly involved in flying. They are the primaries (outer wing), secondaries (inner wing) and tail feathers. Flight feathers are longer, stiffer and less curved than contour feathers, and are aerodynamically shaped.

Numbers of feathers The total number of feathers on a bird varies widely, though it correlates, roughly, with body size. A typical hummingbird, for example, has about 1,000 feathers, whereas a swan has more than 20 times as many. Plumage represents a substantial proportion of a bird's total body weight. The frigatebird, for example, is outweighed by its own feathers. The feathers of a typical songbird are about one-third its body weight.

PLUMAGE CYCLES

As a bird matures, so its plumage changes. In addition, plumage varies from season to season in many species and will, at least once a year, be completely replaced in a process known as molt.

Molting Despite constant care, feathers inevitably wear out. All adult birds molt their feathers at least once a year. The old, worn feather is dropped, or shed, then a new feather grows in its place. When each feather has been shed and replaced, the molt can be said to be complete. This is too clear-cut, however, and in real life, incomplete, overlapping and arrested molts are quite common.

Intricacies of molt Molt of the flight feathers is the most highly organized part of the process. Some species, for example, begin by dropping the outermost primary on each side (to retain balance in the air) and wait until the replacement feathers are about one-third grown before shedding the next outermost, and so on. Others always start with the

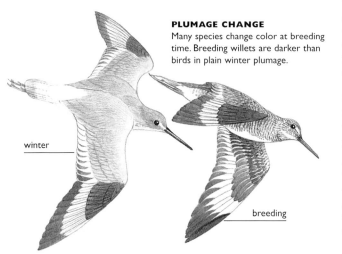

PLUMAGE CHANGE
Many species change color at breeding time. Breeding willets are darker than birds in plain winter plumage.

winter

breeding

winter

summer

BROWN NECKS IN SUMMER
The hind neck of the brown pelican, of North and South America, turns brown prior to nesting in summer.

innermost primary and work outward. Yet other species begin in the middle and work outward on both sides. Most ducks shed all their wing feathers at once.

Juvenile plumage When a bird hatches, it may be nearly naked, as in a typical songbird, or covered in down, like a duckling. In either case, development of the ability to fly is generally the point at which the young bird reaches independence. Juvenile plumage is defined as the first plumage state in which true contour feathers are present, but for practical purposes it can be viewed as the first set of feathers with which flight is possible. Any subsequent plumages between the juvenile plumage and full sexual maturity are referred to as immature plumages.

Plumage cycles In most birds, first breeding marks the point at which an adult cycle of plumages is attained, which will continue throughout life. In many birds, this involves a continuous cycle of two alternating plumages: winter and summer, or breeding and non-breeding. Not all birds breed in summer, however, and some birds court and form pair bonds in their "breeding" plumage but molt out of it before they actually breed.

ON THE WAY TO ADULTHOOD
A well-grown Adélie penguin chick is partway through a molt that will take it into adult plumage.

FLIGHT

Essentially, birds are animals built for flight. Their wings create lift in exactly the same way as the wings of an aircraft. The size and shape of a bird's wing can tell you a great deal about its lifestyle and feeding requirements.

Efficiency and form Just as aircraft are designed with different wing shapes according to their function, so evolution has ensured that the forms of birds' wings exactly suit their lifestyle. In both birds and aircraft, the degree of lift, thrust and maneuverability all depend on the form of the wing and tail.

Wing shape The most significant feature in relation to flight is the wing shape. Generally, a long, narrow wing is more efficient than a short, blunt wing—for purely aerodynamic, non-biological reasons that are well understood by aircraft designers. So birds that spend much time in the air, such as swallows, swifts and migratory shorebirds such as golden-plovers, have long, narrow wings that provide maximum efficiency.

WATERFOWL
Waterfowl fly fast in a direct line, flapping their wings at a steady rate to maintain speed.

VULTURES
Vultures use rising air currents (thermals) to propel them in an upward spiral.

WOODPECKERS
Woodpeckers alternately flap their wings to gain speed and glide to conserve energy.

Acceleration Flapping long wings is much harder work than flapping short ones. Many ground-dwelling birds, such as quail, pheasants and partridges, need flight for little more than escape from predators. What matters for these birds is rapid acceleration; efficiency is less significant because their flights are generally of short duration. The best possible configuration is therefore a short, blunt wing.

Tails Tail shapes also have a bearing on flight performance and vary for similar reasons. A short tail is aerodynamically efficient but a long tail can improve maneuverability.

KINGFISHER AT WORK
A kingfisher's wings are relatively short, allowing it maximum maneuverability as it hunts for fish along rivers and streams.

Modes of flight This close relationship between lifestyle and wing and tail configuration is manifest in most birds. Like fighter aircraft, falcons have narrow, backswept wings that can provide a high level of performance in open skies. Some other raptors, such as accipiters, operate in more cluttered environments, such as woodlands, and rely heavily on surprise. They have broad wings and long tails, which provide them with maximum agility and acceleration. Large birds of prey, such as vultures

and eagles, ride thermals all day to conserve energy. They therefore have little need to flap their wings, which consequently tend to be long and broad, providing maximum lift.

Hummingbirds In contrast to the birds of prey, hummingbirds flap their wings at an incredible speed that requires a high expenditure of energy. Their wings have more in common with helicopter rotor blades than with conventional aircraft wings, and they share many of the helicopter's flight characteristics, especially in the sacrifice of speed and range in return for a significant gain in precision. Like helicopters, hummingbirds can fly backward or forward or hover in midair with almost equal ease.

HABITATS AND NICHES

A bird's habitat is more than just a place: It is a complex web of relationships between the bird species that occupy it, the vegetation, the climate, the food supply and predators. Each habitat has a characteristic array of species, many of them with morphological adaptations to that habitat.

Habitats The habitat of a bird species is often most conveniently expressed in terms of vegetation type—woodland, for example. Birds have come to occupy almost all habitats from frozen wastelands to deserts, and from swamps to dense rain forests.

Ecological niches Bird species have specialized to such an extent in order to survive that not only do they favor a particular habitat but they also prefer a specific slot, or ecological niche, within that habitat. This niche is often

NICHE MARKETS
Insect-eating thornbills occupy different niches in the same area. The striated thornbill (top) feeds in the forest canopy; the brown (middle) in the understory; and the yellow-rumped (bottom) on the ground.

associated with the means of gathering food. One species might forage for insects on the ground, another in tree bark, another on the ground and yet another in flight. These birds occupy the same habitat and share the same basic diet. They differ, however, in the equipment and techniques that they use to obtain their food. These differences define each bird's position—its niche—within its community.

Bills and feet Of all the characteristics that relate to a bird's niche and how it obtains its food, the most obvious are the sizes and shapes of the bill and feet. The fine, pointed bill of the Carolina wren is suited to gleaning insects from underbrush foliage, the straight, stout bill of the wood-pecker is used for hammering tree trunks to remove bark, while the fine, downward-curving bill of the brown creeper serves to probe beneath the bark or into fissures. The great talons of raptors are for gripping large prey, the webbed feet of ducks for swimming, and the long toes of the jacana for walking on water lilies.

THE NUT-CRACKER
The larger parrots and macaws, with their strong, heavy bills, are able to crack open very large seeds and nuts with ease.

Wings and tails Long wings provide economy during flight: Long, pointed wings enable the chimney swift to stay aloft most of the day. Long tails can provide maneuverability and are found on most fly-catching birds.

CARRION-FEEDER
The African marabou stork feeds on carrion, often the leftovers from a lion kill. As it plunges its head into the carcass, its powerful beak tears strips of flesh from the bone.

BIRD BEHAVIOR

The charms of birdsong have long entranced us, inspiring, for example, some of the finest poetry in the English language. Only comparatively recently have we come to realize that these pleasant sounds are part of a complex system of behavior. In fact, birds have some of the most intricate behavior patterns in the animal kingdom. This chapter examines those patterns, looking at the ways in which birds find food and avoid predators, how they attract mates and establish territories and breeding groups, and how they build nests and care for their young. And then there is the puzzle of bird migration—the most amazing mass movement of all living things.

FINDING FOOD

The ability to find a constant food supply is very important to birds, as most cannot store large reserves. Whether they are probing the shoreline for crabs, diving for fish, or searching for seeds in bushes, most birds spend a high proportion of their waking hours in pursuit of food.

MAKING A MEAL OF A RATTLER
The greater roadrunner of the United States and Mexico can take on deadly rattlesnakes, stabbing them with its pointed bill. Normally, the bird kills less challenging prey, such as mice, gophers, lizards, insects, spiders and centipedes.

Bills Bills are basically tools, adapted to suit a feeding behavior. The daggerlike bill of the herons, the pouches of the pelican's bill, the hooked bill of the predatory birds, and the heavy bill of seed-eating parrots and finches are all adaptations to their food.

Fast food It is of great benefit to birds to find food as quickly and economically as possible, especially if they feed in the open where predators lurk. A thrush that has just found a worm will search in the same area more carefully—a good strategy given that worms usually occur in groups. A flycatcher, which eats small insects in the treetops, moves closer to the ground later when large flies are more active, as these yield more energy for the work expended on catching them.

LEARNING CURVE
The blue jay seems to form a mental "search image" based on the most prominent characteristics of its prey. It uses this as a template to filter out excess information.

Techniques Individual birds may develop different feeding skills and concentrate on finding the foods to which they are best adapted. Some gulls may feed on the shore, eating crabs and other invertebrates, while others search for food on farming land, and yet others specialize in waste dumps.

Bird tools Some birds show behavior that includes the use of "tools." Song thrushes use special stones, on which they repeatedly smash snail shells until they break. The woodpecker finch of the Galapagos Islands uses a cactus spine held in the bill to extract grubs from holes in trees.

AVOIDING BEING EATEN
Flocking to safety A lone finch is easy prey to a hawk. It is probably for this reason that many small birds feed in flocks, where they can benefit from the warning provided by more pairs of eyes. Each bird may be able to spend more time feeding and less looking out for predators simply because of the safety in numbers.

Owl-snake The burrowing owl lives in the burrows of ground squirrels, and if confronted by one of these, it utters a call that resembles that of a rattlesnake, thus scaring off the potential predator.

DISPLAYS

In the course of evolution, certain actions by birds have come to have a communicative function. Song, of course, is one such action, but most other communication between birds is visual and often involves plumage displays.

Plumage as display A wide variety of birds have developed plumage colors and patterns that send messages at certain times of the year. The most common manifestation of this is the colorful breeding plumage that many acquire each spring, which often extends to elaborate features that may be used in specific displays. Such features take a variety of forms and usually occur on the most visible parts of the body, especially the head, neck and breast, upper wings or tail. For example, they may be specialized feathers. Male egrets develop elaborate and colorful plumes, and male hummingbirds have iridescent gorgets and crowns that change color as they move. Possibly the most spectacular feather display of all is the male peacock's fanning of his raised upper tail-coverts.

Color and pattern In some cases the combination of color and pattern is particularly important. The male wood duck, for example, has glossy, bright-colored plumage with a sleek crest or hood. This crest can be depressed tightly against its neck and spread to one side to accentuate its appearance. More bizarre features have evolved, purely for display, in other species. The male frigatebird, for example, has a bright red throat pouch which he inflates to attract a mate. Similarly, the neck feathers of some grouse and prairie-chickens can be erected during courtship to reveal large, inflated air sacs with brightly colored skin.

Display behavior Displays are not confined to the appearance of the bird—behavioral factors also come into play. The male peacock performs as he fans his extraordinary tail. Breeding egrets posture to show themselves to best effect. Male wood ducks in the breeding season always parade past the females in the same posture and at the same angle, showing only their best side!

Display flights Sometimes the behavioral component in the display dominates. Displays by raptors, for example, are almost entirely behavioral, and usually involve some kind of demonstration of aerial agility or power. A

TRUMPETING CRANES
Throughout the year, but especially in spring on or near their breeding grounds, common cranes perform a dance in which the birds leap up with raised wings and trumpet loudly.

number of other birds also give display flights, including hummingbirds, woodcock, snipe and larks. These flights are often accompanied by singing.

Why birds display
Most displays, particularly the more elaborate ones, are sexual—that is, they are designed to attract potential mates—and the male bird generally takes the initiative. Males therefore have more colorful plumage and perform most of the display routines (though there are many exceptions).

Other displays There are various other types of display, such as actions of greeting, threat and submission. Some birds, such as the killdeer—a type of plover—use displays to distract predators from their eggs or chicks.

33

SONGS AND CALLS

The joyous sound of birdsong is not only a source of pleasure and inspiration, it is also a valuable aid to field identification, and many birders rely on songs and calls to put a name to the more reclusive species in the field.

How birds sing In birds, as opposed to mammals, the larynx lacks vocal cords. Instead, vocalization is produced by the syrinx, a specialized organ found only in birds that is situated at the base of the windpipe, or trachea. The syrinx is remarkably sophisticated, having two chambers which the bird can use simultaneously to produce extremely complex sounds.

Calls Vocalizations can be divided into calls and songs. In general, songs are used in sexual contexts and calls are used for all other types of vocal communication. There are calls covering most aspects of social behavior, including threat, alarm, flight, begging and so on. Although calls are relatively short and simple, there is evidence that they transmit information about the identity of the calling bird.

Special calls Some species have calls that have specialized functions. Cave-dwelling swifts, for example, emit a series of echolocating clicks when flying in the dark.

CORN BUNTING

The corn bunting has a song that starts with a few slow, chipping notes and ends in a fast jingle, not unlike the jangling of a bunch of keys.

Songs Generally, the male bird does the singing (but there are exceptions) and the songs function as either territorial announcements or as sexual attractants. Although each species has a distinctive song, some birds incorporate mimicry of other species in their repertoires. Experiments show that while some birds are born with their songs, others learn them from their parents. There are a few birds, such as the stork, which seldom vocalize.

Duets Sometimes a song includes contributions from two individuals, usually a mated pair. This is known as duetting and, at times, the co-ordination between the two singers is remarkable.

REED WARBLER
The songs of warblers, such as the great reed warbler, are rich and distinctive, in contrast to their plain plumage.

Bird dialects As with human languages, local dialects occur, with certain characteristics of songs in one population differing from those in other populations. Also, some first-year males sing a little differently from adult birds, and different songs may be sung as the breeding season progresses.

Other sounds Sounds other than songs and calls are also created by birds. This happens in a number of ways.

SONG SPARROW
The song sparrow of North America sings a varied arrangement of chips and trills during summer and spring.

Some species, such as the common snipe, produce loud, distinctive sounds by diving at high speed so that air passes rapidly through stiffened or modified wing and tail feathers. Others, including most grouse and prairie-chickens, use air sacs on the neck to produce loud booming sounds.

TERRITORY AND PAIR FORMATION

For a bird, a desirable territory is an area that provides all that it requires in the way of food, shelter and a nesting site, either for its general survival or for breeding. All territories are defended, usually against other birds of the same species, but also against other species.

Territory types Territories that provide all the necessary resources will be occupied by a pair of birds throughout the breeding season, or even throughout their entire lives. Other territories may be used for particular purposes, notably roosting and feeding. Food may be gathered at a shared foraging site, or pairs may occupy and defend separate feeding territories.

Territories and courtship A variety of resources, the most obvious one being food, attracts females to territories held by males for breeding or specifically for courtship and mating. If a resource is scarce or unevenly distributed, then males with better-quality territories are likely to attract a greater number of females.

Forming a bond Generally, when a female first appears in a male's territory she is greeted as an intruder, but in response to submissive behavior on her part the male stops being aggressive and begins courting her. This may involve intricate social ceremonies.

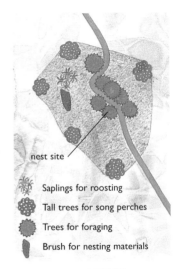

nest site

- 🌸 Saplings for roosting
- 🔴 Tall trees for song perches
- 🟢 Trees for foraging
- 🟤 Brush for nesting materials

SONGBIRD TERRITORY
A typical songbird's territory includes all the resources needed to sustain a breeding attempt. The key indicates the uses of the resources.

COLONIAL BIRDS

Most birds nest individually, but some, such as these Adélie penguins, nest close to each other in large colonies. Each pair will defend the immediate surrounds of the nest.

COURTSHIP GIFTS

Coutship sometimes involves the transfer of a "gift" from one partner to the other, as in the courtship feeding of these sandwich terns.

Courtship feeding, for example, is widespread—it is a means of winning the female, and also reflects her need for extra food during breeding and incubation.

Pair bonds Some birds bond for life; some form new partnerships at the start of each breeding season; and some do not form pairs at all, the male or female mating with a number of partners. Most songbirds form a pair bond for breeding, and the relationship may be resumed in subsequent breeding seasons.

37

NESTS AND EGGS

As soon as a breeding pair has formed, work will begin on building a nest. This will serve as a cradle for the eggs and a temporary home for the developing chicks. Selection of the nest site and building the nest may be undertaken by either sex, either alone or as a pair.

Nest diversity Birds use an amazing range of techniques to create a wide variety of structures. The nest may be elaborate, such as those made by weavers, or it may be a simple scrape in the ground. Some birds build no nest at all, while others create a vast pile. Still others, such as great horned owls, reuse the nests of other species.

Eggs The batch of eggs laid in a single breeding attempt is known as a clutch and may take up to a week to lay. A complete clutch may comprise only a single egg,

as in some seabirds and vultures, or up to a dozen or more in the case of waterfowl.

Incubation The eggs may be incubated by the male, by the female, or by both. The period of incubation varies from a couple of weeks in smaller birds to over eight weeks in gannets, vultures and eagles. Either or both sexes may care for the young.

BALLS OF FLUFF
Barn owl chicks are born naked and helpless, and are fed by both parents. These youngsters have their fluffy coat of down and will soon leave the nest.

Types of chicks In some birds (for example, songbirds and birds of prey), chicks are born blind and helpless. These altricial chicks are fed and cared for by their parents

MOTHER AT NEST
Most birds build cup-shaped nests of twigs and grass firmly wedged into the fork of a tree or bush. This female American goldfinch is about to resume incubating her eggs.

SECONDHAND NESTS
Some birds make their nests in sites taken over from other birds or from mammals. This northern wheatear has used an old rabbit hole for a nest.

until they have developed sufficiently to fledge. This can often be several weeks. In other birds (for example, ducks and gulls), the young are well developed at birth and leave the nest within a day of hatching. These precocial chicks rapidly learn to feed themselves, and the parents provide them only with shelter and protection.

Brood parasites Brood parasites are birds that lay their eggs in the nests of other birds, leaving these eggs to be hatched and the chicks to be reared by the unwitting foster parents.

MIGRATION

Some species of sedentary birds remain in the same geographical area throughout their lives. However, nearly half the world's birds divide their year between two main localities and undertake annual migrations.

Why birds migrate Most migrations result from seasonal fluctuations in the availability of a particular food. In temperate countries, there tends to be more food around in summer and fall than in winter and spring. Winter weather causes a reduction in the amount of food available, and shorter days mean there is less time to gather it.

Flocking together While most birds travel alone, some migrate in flocks of one or more species. The benefits of traveling in flocks

ON THE GO
Swallows make some of the longest migrations of any bird. From North America, the species makes annual journeys of up to 7,000 miles (11,300 km).

include greater protection against predation (particularly for birds that travel during the day), and, for younger migrants, in some cases at least (geese and cranes, for example), being guided by more experienced birds.

Navigation It is thought that most birds navigate by sight, using the Sun to guide them during the day and the stars to lead them at night. Birds also have a built-in "chronometer," or innate time sense, that tells them when it is time to depart, how long the journey will take, and so on. But while these senses and abilities are present from birth, migrants also learn from experience, becoming familiar with territories and fly-ways. They also learn to follow air and sea currents, to use changes in temperature as guides, and to watch the passage of other birds.

Strategies Migration strategies vary. Songbirds often migrate in short hops, while other birds undertake epic nonstop journeys. The greatest globetrotter in terms of distance covered each year is the arctic tern. Terns that breed in the Arctic and North Atlantic overwinter in Antarctica at the opposite side of the globe. The American golden-plover also makes nonstop transoceanic flights of thousands of miles, from the Canadian Atlantic coast to north-eastern South America.

Irruptions Not all movements of birds involve migration. Non-seasonal movements, which are mainly brought about by regular or irregular changes in food supplies, can result in a species appearing in areas well outside its normal range. Such movements are known as irruptions. The snowy owl, for example, visits the United States from the American Arctic regions only when there is a drastic decline in the number of lemmings, its chief prey.

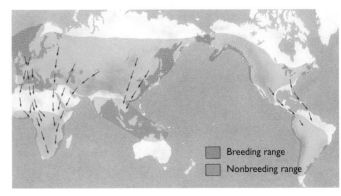

Breeding range
Nonbreeding range

SOUTH FOR THE WINTER
The map brings home the incredible traveling ability of the swallow. This bird breeds commonly across North America (where it is known as the barn swallow), Europe and Asia, and winters in South America, Africa and South-East Asia.

42

THE WORLD OF BIRDS
HUMANS
AND
BIRDS

Through the centuries, people have delighted in observing the activities of the birds around them. Their beauty has always been a source of joy and wonder, and at times a consolation. Birding is a natural extension of this very human interest. Simply watching common song-birds in the back yard is a good start. A pair of binoculars, a field guide, and perhaps a camera, open up new vistas—from witnessing courtship displays in an isolated wetland to observing rare birds of prey riding the thermals over desert hills. This chapter offers practical tips on how to begin your career as a birder, as well as somber information on the ways in which human activity continues to place many species at risk.

BASIC BIRDING

Most of us are birders of a kind, in that we are bound to notice the birds around us from time to time. It is unusual to find a person who cannot tell the difference between a pelican and a hawk, for instance. Really, we are all just a step away from the great enjoyment birding can bring.

BINOCULAR BASICS
When choosing binoculars, size and weight are important considerations, but the pair you buy must also deliver a bright, crisp image at both short and long range.

First steps Start by browsing through bird identification books at home to become familiar with the various groups and species you are likely to come across. The next step is to study an area in your neighborhood, such as a park, using the information in this chapter to help you develop your identification skills. Fairly soon, however, you are likely to want to acquire a complete field guide to the birds of your region. After binoculars, a good field guide will be your most important birding tool. A wide range is available.

Binoculars All binoculars feature a set of numbers such as 7 x 40. The 7 denotes the number of times the bird will be magnified. For birding, select a pair between 7x and 10x.

Brightness and weight The second number that appears on your binoculars—40 in the above example—denotes the diameter of the objective (front) lenses. The larger these are, the more light will enter the binoculars and the brighter the image will be. However, the larger the objective lenses are, the heavier the binoculars will be, a significant consideration when you are out in the field.

Close focus A good pair of birding binoculars should focus on objects that are as close as 14 feet (4.2 m), and the closer they can focus, the better. Some binoculars have a minimum viewing distance of 23 feet (7 m) or more, which is totally impractical for birding.

Going afield For the beginner, it can seem very difficult to even get close to birds. However, as long as you go looking for them within their range and at the right time of year, and keep in mind the following information, you will find that a large number of birds can be located with just a little careful planning.

Approaching birds While some birds may be approached openly, many are timid and will flee at the first hint of danger. It is therefore important to learn to move as silently and unobtrusively as possible when you are waiting at a birding spot.

Field tactics So that you will not alarm birds, move slowly and avoid talking loudly or snapping twigs. Standing still in one spot for some time is often the most effective tactic. Also, try to avoid breaking the horizon line with the outline of your body.

Camouflage
Earth-toned clothes may camouflage you to some extent. Use cover wherever possible: Hide behind vegetation, a rock, or even a car. Remember, however, that the bird's observation skills are far better than yours and it will almost always know you are there!

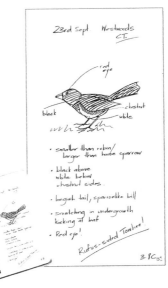

A VISUAL REFERENCE
If you see a bird that you are unable to identify, it's a good idea to make notes and even do a sketch in a notebook. Note the time and place, the kind of habitat and any distinctive features.

45

IDENTIFYING BIRDS

Frequently, novice birders are dismayed by the huge number of species listed in field guides. How can anyone memorize all those birds? The secret is to learn to focus on particular features of the birds you see, thereby becoming proficient in identifying all but the most difficult species.

WINGBARS
Looking at the wingbars helps to distinguish this black-throated green warbler (right) from the Wilson's warbler (left).

Step by step When you are trying to identify a bird, always start by considering what you see in front of you. Describe the bird to yourself and try to draw on information you already have in your head. Keep in mind the following questions.

What family or group does the bird belong to? Most families of birds share certain physical characteristics, and if you can be sure what group a bird belongs to, you are well on your way to identifying the bird.

What size is the bird? The size of a lone bird may be hard to deduce, but try matching it to one you know. Is it bigger or smaller than a robin? Is it similar to the size of a crow?

What is the bird doing? Because different groups of birds demonstrate different behaviors,

what a bird is doing may help to identify it. Is it pecking at the ground, leaf-gleaning in a tree or making short flights to and from an exposed perch? Is it swimming and surface diving?

Is the bird alone or in a group? At certain times of the year, some birds join huge flocks of their own and similar species. Insect-eaters come together to increase foraging efficiency and predator avoidance. Other birds are solitary, except during the breeding season.

What are the distinguishing features?

To identify a species you have to learn to recognize its field marks, the characteristics of a species that, taken together, distinguish that bird from others. Usually they are plumage features. Pay particular attention to the following parts of the bird:
• eyebrow (supercilium)
• rump

TAIL FEATHERS
The outer tail feathers are field marks in many species. Frequently the distinguishing mark is a lighter tip or sides.

• outer tail feathers
• wingbars

Always bear in mind that patterns are more significant than colors.

Where are you? Also, what time of year is it? What kind of habitat are you in? Write down in your notebook where you are, what time of year and day it is,

EYE MARKINGS
The pattern of the eyebrow (supercilium) or eye-ring often distinguishes a species, as with the black-capped vireo (left), the northern wheatear (center), and the white-throated sparrow (right).

and what kind of habitat the bird is in. It is important that you have noted these details accurately, as they may help you to confirm a sighting. Many birds are common only within a particular range at particular times of year and favor a specific habitat. Most field guides give an indication of the distributions of species and their habitat preferences.

PHOTOGRAPHING BIRDS

The sense of satisfaction achieved by taking a good color slide or print of a bird—perfectly composed, accurately exposed, crackling sharp, and with good saturated colors—is enormous, and most birders want to try their hand at capturing their quarry on film at some time.

LENSES
Mirror lenses (top) are more compact than other lenses, whereas zoom lenses (center) provide increased flexibility. At bottom is a 600 mm lens.

Cameras For birding, the recommended style and format is a single lens reflex (SLR) camera that uses 35 mm film, preferably one with automatic exposure control and focusing capability.

Focal length The most important variable to consider when choosing a lens for bird photography is its focal length. Usually expressed in millimeters, this is what governs the size of the image of the bird on the film. With a 35 mm camera, you can roughly equate this with the magnification of your binoculars by dividing the focal length of the lens by 50: A 400 mm lens, for example, is roughly the equivalent of 8x binoculars. The greater the focal length, the harder it is to maintain focus and to "target" your bird in the finder. Beyond about 400 mm you will need to use a tripod to get worthwhile results.

The f-stop The second critical parameter is the f-stop, which measures the light-gathering capability of the lens. The smaller the number, the wider the lens opens, the more light is let into the camera, and the quicker the

image will be processed. An f4 lens is therefore better (that is, faster) than an f5.6. On the other hand, the smaller the number, the bigger and heavier the lens, and the more expensive.

To get results as good as this shot of a green-cheeked Amazon parrot requires a not insignificant investment of time, money and patience.

Zoom and mirror lenses

Zoom lenses are those in which the focal length is variable (75 to 125 mm is a typical range). Mirror lenses are much smaller, lighter and more compact than normal telephoto lenses, but their f-stop is fixed. Such considerations are not all that important in bird photography, however, as you will usually find yourself operating the lens at maximum zoom, in order to get as close as possible to the bird, and with the aperture wide open, in order to record the image as quickly as possible.

Film The most important difference in film types is in speed. High speed films (indicated by higher numbers) allow you to use a faster shutter speed and are therefore better for catching birds in motion, but they tend to give you grainier pictures. If you want the very best results, have your exposed film processed by a custom lab rather than by the corner drugstore.

WHICH CAMERA?
Always use an SLR camera for bird photography. Rangefinder cameras do not allow you to change lenses, so you cannot use a telephoto lens.

BIRDS UNDER THREAT

More than a thousand bird species are faced with extinction today, according to Bird Life International. In fact, the situation is worse than even this figure implies, for many more are declining or are potentially vulnerable and could soon be threatened with extinction too.

A sad record About 100 birds, mostly island species, have become extinct in the past 400 years. Species have always died out, but the big difference between the species that have become extinct in historical times and those that disappeared in prehistoric times is that recent extinctions can be attributed almost wholly to the activities of human beings.

Why birds are endangered
The greatest cause of extinctions has been the effect of introduced species on island birds. The greatest overall threat today, however, is undoubtedly habitat destruction, which affects both island and continental species.

Habitats at risk
Almost all major habitat types have been affected by encroachment. Grasslands have been plowed or overgrazed by livestock; wetlands have been

SIBERIAN CRANE
The beautiful Siberian crane is highly endangered, mainly because of the loss of its wintering grounds in southern Asia. Its survival depends on the conservation of these areas.

endangered

least concern

declining or potentially threatened

STATUS REPORT
The precarious status of the world's birds is shown in this pie chart. About 11 percent of the world's birds are regarded as threatened.

drained; tropical rain forests have been cut down and cleared. It is no coincidence that the type of habitat that is home to the highest number of threatened species is tropical rain forest.

Introduced species Introduced species, especially predators such as cats, rats and mongooses, have been the main cause of extinction of island birds. Many of these birds evolved without any predator pressure and were unable to cope with introduced aliens. Rabbits and goats create adverse changes by eating vegetation.

Other factors Hunting for food has caused the extinction of some bird species, mainly on islands.

TEN ENDANGERED BIRDS*

BERMUDA PETREL
BLUE-THROATED MACAW
GIANT KINGBIRD
JAVAN HAWK-EAGLE
LORD HOWE RAIL
ST HELENA PLOVER
SIBERIAN CRANE
TAKAHE
WHITE-THROATED JAY
WHOOPING CRANE

* An endangered bird has a 20 percent chance of becoming extinct in the next 20 years.

The wild-bird trade is a growing threat to birds, particularly for some sought-after species of parrot. Pesticides and pollution of the environment threaten birds by the death of individuals through ingesting toxic chemicals or by reducing breeding success.

Conservation efforts Different species have different conservation needs, but some combination of preserving habitats, eliminating introduced species, curbing hunting, controlling trade and preventing pollution will help to ensure the survival of threatened species. Many countries have already taken such measures. Other efforts can profitably be focused on key sites where several threatened species occur together. If these sites can be preserved, we shall be making a major contribution to maintaining the Earth's biological diversity.

PART TWO

KINDS OF BIRDS

WATERBIRDS

Waterbirds are a diverse group, ranging from certain types of ducks that spend almost all their time on lakes and ponds, to ibises, some species of which actually spend most of their time away from water. In general, though, the birds in this chapter inhabit an environment of lakes, swamps, mangroves, lagoons and other stretches of water. Their bodies and habits reflect this. Long-legged herons and spoonbills wade into deep water for food; while small, narrow-bodied rails stick to the reedbeds on the margins. Wetlands are fragile places, too, and are easily harmed by human action. Any discussion of waterbirds will therefore inevitably touch on threats to their world.

DIVERS (LOONS)

Divers (known as loons in North America) are superbly streamlined aquatic birds about the size of a duck. They constitute the family Gaviidae, which makes up the order Gaviiformes. Shy by nature, they inhabit lakes in northern forests and tundra. Their wild hollering and yodeling calls, audible for several miles, conjure up for many people the essence of these lonely northern wildernesses.

Characteristics Divers are 26 to 33 inches (66–84 cm) long. In winter they are a rather uniform sooty gray above and white below, and species are hard to tell apart, but for the breeding season their plumage is adorned with elaborate patterns. The red-throated diver *Gavia stellata* acquires a rufous patch on the throat and a pattern of black-and-white lines on the hind-neck. The black-throated diver *G. arctica* has black-and-white lines on the side of the neck

and four areas checkered in white on its black back. The great northern diver *G. immer* of Iceland and North America, and the white-billed diver *G. adamsii* of Arctic North America and Siberia, are mostly black with their back decorated by square white patches like a chessboard.

Feeding They travel rapidly under water in pursuit of fish, and in extreme cases can dive to a depth of 230 feet (70 m).

TELLING LOONS APART
All loons are dark above and white below. The common loon (left) has a large, angular head and a stout, straightish bill. These are among the features that distinguish it from the smaller Pacific loon (right).

Reproduction As they are unable to walk properly, divers place their nest at the lake's edge, allowing the bird to slip easily into the water. Most nest sites are on

ORDER GAVIIFORMES
Divers (loons) are found in far northern latitudes, including the high Arctic tundra and the icy seas nearby.

flies to larger lakes or out to sea for food. The other species prefer lakes large enough to satisfy the family's needs until the young fledge at 10 to 12 weeks of age.

Habitat Loons live in ponds and lakes in northern North America, Siberia, Greenland, Iceland and northern Europe. They winter at sea, staying well off the coasts.

CLASSIFICATION

ORDER GAVIIFORMES
1 FAMILY • 1 GENUS • 5 SPECIES
FAMILY GAVIIDAE

peninsulas or small islands, and nests are usually just shallow scrapes in the boggy ground. The female lays just two eggs on average, which are incubated for a month. The young are clad with sooty brown down and have two successive downy plumages. They can swim and dive at once, but the young of larger species prefer to ride on their parents' back at first. The red-throated diver breeds mainly in small remote ponds and

Three species of divers, clockwise from right: the great northern, the black-throated (winter and summer plumage) and the red-throated (winter and summer).

GREBES AND DABCHICKS

Slim, elegant and adorned with crest and ruff, some grebes are considered to be the most fascinating birds on the lake. The smaller grebes, often called dabchicks, are less spectacular, resembling ducklings with a pointed bill. These birds are supremely well adapted for life on water; they even build floating nests. They make up the single-family order Podicipediformes.

Characteristics The sexes look alike. In length, birds range from 9½ to 11 inches (24–28 cm) for the least grebe *Tachybaptus dominicus* to 27 inches (70 cm) for the great grebe *Podiceps major*. Grebes have flexible, compressed feet, with semi-webbed toes, which can work almost like a propeller, giving great maneuverability and speed when the birds pursue prey in the water. Grebes usually avoid danger by diving, so flying is unnecessary for their daily life and they can therefore molt all wing feathers at the same time. To become airborne, the birds need a running start. They fly fast, but, unable to make fast turns, may be vulnerable to birds of prey and so prefer to migrate at night.

Feeding Small and dumpy grebes live among water reeds, taking water insects and making quick darts for small fish; such grebes exist worldwide, even in small creeks and ephemeral ponds. Large, streamlined grebes prefer larger lakes, because they are specialized for taking fish. The elegant western grebe *Aechmorphorus occidentalis* can spear fish with its slender bill.

Other dumpy and small-billed grebes are specialized to pick tiny arthropods from among the waterweeds. While fish-stalking grebes feed singly, the latter type are social feeders.

Reproduction The courtship rituals of grebes are complex. Especially in the larger species the two partners often face each other for long bouts of mutual head-shaking. They also "dance," maintaining their bodies almost vertically out of the water, or they rush side by side in upright positions. Their nests are floating platforms of plant material, usually concealed among reeds. The chicks can swim at once, but being sensitive to cold water they spend most of the time under their parents' wings.

Habitat Grebes spend almost their entire lives in water. Some are sedentary, spending winter and summer on the same stretch of water, but most migrate. Northern Hemisphere species spend the winter on icefree lakes or at sea.

ORDER PODICIPEDIFORMES
Grebes have a worldwide distribution, except for the extreme north and south and some islands.

The little grebe Tachybaptus ruficollis, *also known as the dabchick, feeds mainly on insects and their larvae.*

HERONS

Within the heron family—Ardeidae—of the order Ciconiiformes, there are three main types: typical herons; night herons; and bitterns. Typical herons are discussed here. They are long-legged wading birds, and most have a long neck with a powerful bill designed for stabbing prey.

Characteristics Most typical herons are simple variations on a theme. They vary in size from the rufous heron *Ardeola rufiventris* to the giant goliath heron *Ardea goliath*; they are monochrome (white, black, gray) or a mix of two or more colors including rufous, green, maroon and gray.

CLASSIFICATION

ORDER
CICONIIFORMES
7 FAMILIES
48 GENERA
117 SPECIES
FAMILY ARDEIDAE

GREEN HERON
The green heron *Butorides virescens* hunches quietly at the side of ponds and marshes, waiting for fish. It lives in North America.

Feeding Prey includes fish, amphibians and insects. Some herons feed by standing still and waiting for prey to come to them, while others actively pursue their prey by running or by flying and pouncing onto prey on the surface of the water.

Reproduction During the breeding season, some herons sport special filamentous feathers called "aigrettes." Birds nest in

GREAT EGRET

The great egret *Egretta alba* inhabits freshwater wetlands and coastal waters worldwide, but particularly in the Southern Hemisphere. It was once hunted for its head feathers, which were used to decorate women's hats.

ORDER CICONIIFORMES

The order, which includes herons, bitterns, storks, ibises and spoonbills, is distributed virtually worldwide.

colonies, which may include several other species of waterbirds. For nests, the majority of species construct platforms of sticks in trees or reed beds.

Habitat Herons live in wetlands, shallow waters and grasslands all over the world. Over several decades the cattle egret *Bubulcus ibis*, which once occurred naturally only in Africa and Asia, has successfully invaded most regions of the globe. As is the case with many waterbirds, the draining of wetlands is a major threat.

CATTLE EGRET

Only 50 years ago, the cattle egret *Bubulcus ibis* was uncommon outside its home of Africa and Asia. Today it is perhaps the best known heron, found in most parts of the world. These egrets riding on the backs of cattle or following the plow is a typical sight in many agricultural regions.

CLASSIFICATION

ORDER
CICONIIFORMES
7 FAMILIES
48 GENERA
117 SPECIES
FAMILY ARDEIDAE

PLUMAGE CHANGE
The cattle egret is white most of the year, but this changes at the start of the breeding season. Buff plumes appear on the head, chest and back; the bill becomes reddish; and the legs change color to orange.

"heavy-jowled" look. For most of the year, cattle egrets are white overall with dark legs and a yellow bill.

such as buffalo, giraffe and elephant, but nowadays their link with domestic stock, such as cattle and horses, and their habit of following plows have assisted their near-cosmopolitan spread.

Characteristics The cattle egret is a stocky bird between 18 and 21 inches (45.5–53.5 cm) in length and with a distinctive

Feeding This egret has specialized its feeding behavior to benefit from catching insects disturbed by the grazing of large animals. This habit must have developed in association with wild animals

Reproduction The nest is a platform of sticks in a tree or reed bed, often with other herons. Two to six pale blue eggs are laid.

BITTERN

The Eurasian bittern *Botaurus stellaris* is a mysterious bird of dense reed beds, and a master of disguise. If you are lucky enough to encounter one closely, it will try to make itself less visible by "sky-pointing"—stretching its neck and pointing its bill upward—and swaying with the movement of the reeds, its eyes swiveled forward to keep track of the intruder.

BLENDING IN
Bitterns depend on camouflage rather than flight to avoid predators. If startled, a bittern will adopt this "sky-pointing" posture, trying to blend in with the reeds and the other thin vertical vegetation of its home.

Characteristics The bittern is about 25 to 31 inches long (64–80 cm) and golden brown in color with blackish stripes and bars. The drab plumage provides excellent camouflage among marsh plants. Bitterns have a curious adaptation whereby the eyes are placed widely on the head, which allows them to see across a wide field of vision even when sky-pointing. In spring, the male "booms" like a foghorn, audible at a distance of more than 3 miles (5 km), mostly between dusk and dawn.

Feeding Bitterns walk the floor of reed beds looking for small fish, frogs, insects and spiders.

Reproduction Males are often polygamous and may mate with up to five females. The nest is a platform of dead reeds.

Habitat Bitterns are birds of freshwater marshes and similar places with dense vegetation and tall reeds.

CLASSIFICATION

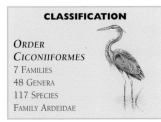

ORDER
CICONIIFORMES
7 FAMILIES
48 GENERA
117 SPECIES
FAMILY ARDEIDAE

STORKS

Storks are known through tales about just one of the 17 species. The white stork *Ciconia ciconia* of Eurasia is regarded as a bringer of fertility and prosperity. But inspiring as this species is, other members of the stork family are also intriguing.

PAINTED STORK
The painted stork *Mycteria leucocephala* is a large, colorful Asian stork commonly seen in marshland reserves.

Characteristics Storks are long-legged, long-necked wading birds. Plumage is mainly some combination of black, white and gray. The legs and bills are bright red. One unusual variation is the shoebill *Balaeniceps rex* of African wetlands, which has a huge, clog-shaped bill for catching slippery lungfish. The white stork, a more typical species, is about 39 to 45 inches (100–115 cm) long. These birds start to migrate to Africa each year at the end of summer, congregating at the Bosporus in flocks of thousands in early fall, an amazing sight.

Feeding Storks eat a variety of foods, including fish, insects, amphibians, crustaceans, small mammals and carrion. Two African openbill storks (genus *Anastomas*) have an unusual adaptation—a bill with a large gap down the sides (hence the bird's common name), which is used to extract the meat from large freshwater snails.

Reproduction Storks have complicated and elaborate courtship displays, which they perform conspicuously. White storks mate for life and build massive nests of huge piles of branches. These are built on rooftops and may be used by the same pair year after year. Both

WHITE STORK

The white stork is probably the most widely known bird in Europe—and for good reason. It often builds its massive nests on buildings in urban areas. It feeds on large insects, voles and frogs.

parents feed the young. The Australasian jabiru *Ephippior-hynchus asiaticus* provides more than food for its offspring; in hot weather it regurgitates water over the chicks to cool them down.

Habitat There are storks in most temperate and tropical parts of the world. The majority of species frequent marshes, estuaries, rivers and creeks, although some storks prefer drier country.

IBISES

Like storks and herons, ibises are another successful family in the order Ciconiiformes that has radiated into most habitats and can be recognized by most people. They are strongly linked with wetlands, although some species prefer dry areas.

WHITE IBIS

The white ibis *Eudocimus albus* inhabits coastal saltmarshes and mangrove swamps and lagoons in the southern United States and in Central and South America.

Characteristics Ibises are wading birds 21 to 25 inches (53–64 cm) long, with long legs and a long, downward-curving bill. Plumage is mainly black, brown or white Their rapid, shallow wingbeats are interspersed with glides, and they hold their neck outstretched.

CLASSIFICATION

ORDER
CICONIIFORMES
7 FAMILIES
48 GENERA
117 SPECIES
FAMILY THRESKIORNITHIDAE

Feeding Ibises use their down-curving bill with a probing feeding action to forage for their water-dwelling diet of mollusks, amphibians and fish.

Habitat Most species live in wetlands, often in tightly packed colonies of thousands of birds. Some species inhabit dry areas, such as forests.

SPOONBILLS

Spoonbills belong to the same family as ibises, share many of their characteristics, and have a similar distribution in the world's temperate and tropical regions. It is these birds' distinctive spoon-shaped bills—specialized for feeding—that set them apart, making them one of the easiest bird groups to identify.

CLASSIFICATION

ORDER
CICONIIFORMES
7 FAMILIES
48 GENERA
117 SPECIES
FAMILY THRESKIORNITHIDAE

The elegant roseate spoonbill Ajaia ajaja *is found in wetlands in South and Central America and the southeast United States.*

Characteristics Like the ibises, plumage tends to be black, brown or white, although red and pink coloration also occurs. The long legs may be red or black. The spoon-shaped bill is a unique adaptation to fishing by touch in shallow water.

Feeding The birds sweep their slightly open bills through the water to catch aquatic life, including small fish, crustaceans, mollusks and marine invertebates.

Vegetation may also be eaten.

Reproduction Spoonbills breed in colonies, building nests of small branches in trees or on the ground in reedbeds.

Habitat They live in marshes and coastal waters.

FLAMINGOS

The bright pink of the flamingo's feathers and the strongly hooked bill instantly identify these birds. At first sight flamingos look strange and awkward because their necks and legs are longer in proportion to their bodies than in other birds, but their beauty and grace are soon revealed.

Characteristics Flamingos are very long-legged and long-necked wading birds. The unique, crooked bill is perfectly adapted for filter feeding. Plumage is a combination of pink, red and white. The largest species is the greater flamingo *Phoenicopteris ruber,* which has a total length of 55 inches (140 cm) and weighs between about 4 and 9 pounds (2.1–4.1 kg); the smallest, the lesser flamingo *Phoenicopteris minor,* is about 40 inches (100 cm) in length and weighs just over 4 pounds (1.9 kg).

Feeding To feed, flamingos drag their bills upside down through the water. The upper mandible is lined with rows of slits, and the tongue is covered with fine toothlike projections. The bill is opened and then, as the mandible is closed, water and mud are pumped out through the bill-slits. The residue probably contains a

FILTER FEEDERS
The long legs and strange bill of the flamingo are adaptations for feeding. Birds wade through brackish waters, using the bill to filter out food.

mixture of microscopic food, including algae and aquatic invertebrates, which is swallowed. Lesser flamingos, of southern

Africa, commonly feed by night in waters so deep that the birds swim rather than wade.

Reproduction Flamingos nest on lakes in shallow mud-cups scraped together so that they project above the water level. Only one egg is laid, and it takes about 30 days to hatch. The young birds leave the nests and herd together

The flight silhouette of the greater flamingo is unmistakable.

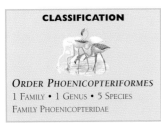

in large creches, and are able to run and swim well at an early age.

Habitat Flamingos are or were found on every continent, although only fossils are present now in Australasia. They seem to prefer salty or brackish waters, frequenting shallow saline or alkaline lakes, lagoons and river deltas.

Well-known species The best known species is the greater flamingo of Eurasia, Africa and Central and southern America; it occasionally wanders from the Caribbean islands to Florida. The females are similar in plumage to the males, but are up to 20 percent smaller. Juveniles are easy to pick out by their gray-brown plumage and brown legs, as well as by their smaller size. Colonies of flamingos

ORDER PHOENICOPTERIFORMES
Flamingos are found on all continents except Australia and Antarctica.

usually consist of thousands of pairs, established in large wetlands far from human disturbance and inaccessible to terrestrial predators such as foxes.

CRANES

Found in North America, Europe, Asia, Africa and Australia, the crane family (Gruidae), of the order Gruiformes, includes 15 species of large wading birds. Cranes are best known for their loud calls, spectacular courtship dances, monogamy and the care they lavish on their young. Cranes are symbols of long life and good luck in the Orient.

CROWNED CRANE

The distinctive crest and the habit of roosting in trees are but two of the features that set the crowned crane *Balearica pavonina* apart from other cranes. This elegant species is found in Africa, from Senegal to central Ethiopia, northern Uganda and northwest Kenya.

CLOSE RELATIVES

Limpkins Closely related to cranes are the water-loving limpkins of the family Aramidae. There is one species *Aramus guarauna*, found in the tropics. It uses its long curved bill to extract snails from their shells.

Trumpeters The trumpeters of the family Psophiidae are also close relatives of cranes; they even have crane-like courtship dances. These South American forest birds have soft feathers and short curved bills.

CLASSIFICATION

ORDER
GRUIFORMES
12 FAMILIES
61 GENERA
220 SPECIES
FAMILY GRUIDAE

Characteristics Cranes are long-necked and long-legged. Plumage is mainly gray or white, with colored plumes or bare skin.

ORDER GRUIFORMES
Members of this order, which includes cranes and rails, are found in most parts of the world.

Feeding Cranes forage for a wide variety of food on dry land and in shallow water.

Reproduction The elaborate courtship dances include loud trumpeting calls. A platform nest is constructed in shallow water, and typically two eggs are laid. Both sexes assist in incubation and care of the young; chicks remain with their parents until the start of the next breeding period.

Habitat They inhabit wetlands and grasslands worldwide. Destruction of habitat has eliminated many species from much of their former range. Seven species of cranes are listed as endangered.

BLUE CRANE
The blue crane *Arthropoides paradisea* occurs in southern Africa, where it frequents dry grasslands, although it prefers to roost and nest in wetlands. In some districts it has colonized farming land.

Waterbirds

71

THE SIBERIAN CRANE'S DANCE

The rare Siberian crane *Grus leucogeranus* is undoubtedly one of the most majestic animals on the planet. For millennia, the wetlands of northern Siberia have been home to these enormous white birds with red faces. Like all cranes, they perform an elaborate courtship display.

With the pair standing side-by-side, the male (on the left) initiates the mating dance by bowing his head.

The male's head movements become more rapid; the female does not respond yet.

After bowing, the male stretches his wings and utters a lengthy cry. The female responds with a call of high-pitched double notes.

The male, head stretched back, then imitates the female's call in a lower pitch. During the dance, both birds shake their heads vertically.

RAILS

Perhaps the best known family within the order Gruiformes is the Rallidae. There are 133 species of rails, gallinules or moorhens, and coots, although 14 species are probably extinct. Of all living groups of birds, the rails are the most likely to lose the ability to fly.

Characteristics Rails are small to medium-sized birds with long legs, suited to their wetland habitats. Their wings are short and rounded, reflecting their ground-living habits. Some species—notably those on islands—have lost the ability to fly. They are secretive, cautious birds.

Feeding A wide variety of food is consumed, including insects, amphibians, nestling birds and small mammals.

Reproduction Nests of reed stems are hidden among vegetation. The moorhen *Gallinula chloropus* has an unusual breeding biology—the young of an earlier brood help their parents in raising a subsequent brood.

Habitat Almost every major wetland on all continents and many islands is home to a species of rail, gallinule or coot. The absence of terrestrial predators led to many island species becoming flightless. The introduction of predators in relatively recent times has seen the extinction of a number of species.

PURPLE GALLINULE
The purple gallinule
Porphyrio martinica,
of North and South
America, has enormous
feet which allow it to
walk on lily pads.

ISLAND RAILS
Lack of predators allowed many island rails to be flightless. Rails are born with relatively tiny wings, as the skeleton shows. Flightless species retain these proportions into adulthood.

CLASSIFICATION

ORDER
GRUIFORMES
12 FAMILIES
61 GENERA
220 SPECIES
FAMILY RALLIDAE

Well-known species The moorhen is a truly cosmopolitan species, occurring all over the world except in Australia, where it is replaced by a very closely related species. It is a highly adaptable bird and can be found in cities, suburbs and parks, as long as there is water with some reed vegetation as cover. Moorhens are usually solitary, but sometimes form small groups during the winter. They feed while walking along the shores of ponds or while swimming. When swimming or walking, the tail is held high and jerked incessantly.

MOORHEN
Almost every kind of freshwater habitat is home to the moorhen. An adult (with red beak) and juvenile are shown here.

SWANS

Collectively known as waterfowl, swans, ducks and geese are among the most beautiful of all birds. Connections between these birds and humans reach far back in time—they were among the first animals to be farmed for meat and eggs. Largest of the waterfowl, the eight species of swans are indigenous to every continent except Africa and Antarctica.

Characteristics Swans are large waterfowl with long necks and flattened, broad, rather spatulate bills. They have dense, waterproof feathers. Of all birds thus far examined, the tundra (whistling) swan *Cygnus colombianus* has the greatest number of feathers—more than 25,000—most of which are on the head and neck. Swans make a variety of sounds, including trumpeting, hissing and snorting, and not even the so-called mute swan *C. olor* is totally mute. They are completely at home on the water, their size and webbed feet making them ungainly on land.

MUTE SWAN
The young of mute swans are dull gray until they molt into the white adult plumage. Native to temperate Eurasia, these birds have been introduced to parts of North America, South Africa and Australia because of their grace and beauty.

Feeding Swans eat submerged water plants—upending to reach shoots on the bottom—as well as grass and the stubble of crops.

ORDER ANSERIFORMES
This order, which includes the swans, geese, ducks and screamers, is found everywhere, except Antarctica.

Reproduction Swans usually mate for life. Most build huge nests, and that of the trumpeter swan *C. buccinator* of North America may be a floating structure. Both sexes care for the young (cygnets). Several species carry cygnets on their back.

Habitat Swans inhabit freshwater and brackish rivers, lakes and marshes; also estuaries.

Well-known species Mute swans are familiar and graceful residents of parks, ponds and rivers in many countries. They are large birds, between 57 and 63 inches (145–160 cm) in length. If you see a pair, look at the black knob above the bill: The bird with the largest is the male. The males can fight fiercely in territorial disputes, sometimes until death.

CLASSIFICATION

ORDER ANSERIFORMES
2 FAMILIES • 51 GENERA
c. 160 SPECIES • FAMILY ANATIDAE

WHOOPER AND BEWICK'S
Whooper swans *Cygnus cygnus* are sometimes found grazing in pastures together with the very similar Bewick's swans *C. columbianus* (two birds at center).

77

GEESE

Geese are part of the large and diverse Anatidae family of waterfowl. The 15 species of true geese are highly gregarious and are confined to the Northern Hemisphere, with most birds breeding in Arctic or subarctic latitudes.

Characteristics

Geese are medium-sized waterfowl with shorter bills than ducks and swans. Most, but not all, are somberly colored. True geese are not sexually dimorphic, but the lesser snow goose *Anser caerulescens* has a distinct dark color morph known as the blue goose, once considered a separate species. The Canada goose *Branta canadensis* has up to about a dozen races of varying sizes. Geese can

SNOW GOOSE
The snow goose nests in colonies of thousands of pairs in the Arctic tundra. They fly south for the winter, some as far as the Gulf of Mexico.

be long-lived, and some birds have reached about 50 years of age. The magpie goose *Anseranas semipalmata* of northern Australia is not a true goose: a gradual wing molt, long toes only partially webbed, polygamous breeding and adult feeding of its young are some of the characteristics that set it apart. The Cape Barren goose *Cereopsis novaehollandiae*, also of Australia, may represent a transitional link to the true geese of the Northern Hemisphere.

Feeding True geese graze on land plants and spend a lot of time ashore. Aquatic invertebrates, however, are an important food source for their goslings.

Reproduction Geese generally mate for life. Nests are usually rudimentary—a depression in the ground lined with down. Some

species, such as the snow goose, nest in large colonies.

Habitat Geese inhabit wetlands, grasslands and agricultural land; several northern species, such as the pink-footed goose *Anser brachyrhynchus*, as well as the snow goose,

CANADA GOOSE
The Canada goose is indigenous to the Arctic and temperate North America, and has been introduced elsewhere, including Europe.

breed on Arctic tundra and fly south to winter on marshes and farming land.

Well-known species Perhaps the most familiar goose to most North Americans, the Canada goose is famous for its geographic variation—some of the largest subspecies are nearly twice as big

FORMATION FLIERS
Their long, broad wings and powerful breast muscles allow geese to fly strongly. The distinctive V-formation aids streamlining.

as the smallest. From eight to eleven subspecies are generally recognized. In general, the smaller races (known as "cackling geese"), give higher-pitched, yelping or cackling calls, and the larger birds (known as "honkers") give more long-drawn-out honking calls. Whatever their size, all Canada geese have the diagnostic white "chinstrap" and are varying shades of brownish below.

Ducks

Ducks make up a large part of the Anatidae family. There are several groups, but the two discussed here are the largest—the perching ducks, which are more arboreal than other Anatidae members, and the dabbling ducks, perhaps the most familiar. Other types of ducks include pochards, eiders, steamer ducks, sea ducks and stifftails.

SHOVELERS

The large, shovel-like bill makes the shoveler *Anas clypeata* one of the most distinctive of dabblers. It swings its bill from side to side just under the water's surface. The comblike teeth in the bill strain out food.

Characteristics Perhaps the most distictive feature of ducks is the broad, flattish bill, with which they sift water and mud to obtain food. With comparatively short legs and strongly webbed front toes, they are excellent swimmers. While a number of species are dull and nondescript, many others are brightly colored and patterned. Males are generally more ornate and vividly colored than females. Drakes of the American wood duck *Aix sponsa* and Asian mandarin duck *A. galericulata* have such complex patterns and bright colors that they are considered to be among the most beautiful of birds. Perching ducks vary widely, ranging in weight from a mere 8 ounces to 22 pounds (230 g–10 kg).

Also known as river or puddle ducks, dabbling ducks include the mallard, wigeons, pintail, shovelers and many teal. An iridescent, metallic, mirrorlike speculum on the wing secondaries is typical of both sexes of most species in the large *Anas* genus.

UPENDING
The best way to get the juiciest parts of water plants is to upend, like this pair of mallards.

CLASSIFICATION

ORDER ANSERIFORMES
2 FAMILIES • 51 GENERA
C. 160 SPECIES • FAMILY ANATIDAE

Feeding Most ducks are omnivorous, eating both plant material and tiny marine animals. Some also catch small fish, while others are wholly vegetarian.

Reproduction The nests of dabbling ducks are generally a cup of leaves and grass on the ground, lined with down. Perching ducks nest in tree holes. The young, like all ducks, are precocial and able to feed on their own as soon as they are out of the egg and dry.

Habitat Dabbling ducks prefer freshwater habitats, but may also frequent salt water. Perching ducks are wet forest-dwellers.

Well-known species The most widespread, versatile and numerous of the dabbling ducks, the mallard *Anas platyrhynchos*, occurs naturally across much of the Northern Hemisphere, but it has been widely introduced elsewhere. This is of some concern because the mallard hybridizes freely with local species, which compromises the indigenous birds' genetic integrity. The typical male has a green head, white neck band and mahogany breast; females are dull and mottled. Mallards are the ancestors of most breeds of domestic or farmyard ducks.

A female green-winged teal Anas crecca *leads its young to water.*

WOOD DUCK

That the wood duck *Aix sponsa* is now common in much of eastern North America is a tribute to a highly successful conservation policy. Early in the twentieth century, wood ducks were threatened with extinction through over-hunting, drainage of wetlands and felling of forests. Their rarity led to a moratorium on hunting for 23 years, from 1918 to 1941, and a program of close habitat management.

CLASSIFICATION

ORDER ANSERIFORMES
2 FAMILIES • 51 GENERA
c. 160 SPECIES • FAMILY ANATIDAE

Characteristics The wood duck is between 17 and 19 inches (43–48 cm) in length. The ornate male is unmistakable for much of the year. After nesting he molts into a drab female-like plumage but keeps his distinctive red bill. Field marks of the female are her bushy pointed crest and her bold white eye-ring.

Reproduction Wood ducks nest in tree cavities.

Habitat These are birds of forested wetlands. Tree clearance in some areas has been overcome by the provision of nesting boxes.

Perched on a tree branch, a male wood duck preens itself.

SHELDUCK

Shelducks *Tadorna tadorna* are gooselike birds which breed in much of coastal Eurasia, spending winters in Africa and parts of Asia. In July and August, huge numbers of these birds from a large area of Europe migrate to a selected number of sites—such as Germany's Wadden Sea—to molt. After the wing feathers are fully regrown, the birds disperse again to their original haunts.

MATCHING PLUMAGE
Unlike most ducks, males and female shelducks have identical—and very colorful—plumage; the males have a red knob on the forehead. The downy young are beautifully black and white, and juveniles are grayish above and white below.

Characteristics Shelducks are the size of a goose and look white and black from a distance, but appear surprisingly colorful close up. Males are larger than females and have a large red knob on the forehead.

CLASSIFICATION

ORDER ANSERIFORMES
2 FAMILIES • 51 GENERA
C. 160 SPECIES • FAMILY ANATIDAE

Feeding Food is mainly small mollusks, crustaceans and insects; some vegetable matter is also eaten.

Reproduction Shelducks breed in holes, preferably rabbit burrows. If these are not available, other sheltered places are chosen, such as old barns or hollow trees.

Habitat These are birds of estuaries and shallow seas.

DIVING DUCKS

Pochards and stifftails are ducks with excellent
diving abilities. Pochards are rather closely related
to the dabbling ducks. The stifftails, named for
their distinctive stiff tails, are so adapted to an
aquatic, diving lifestyle that they can barely walk.

RUDDY DUCK
When the ruddy duck
Oxyura jamaicensis
dives, it sinks slowly
beneath the surface,
barely leaving a ripple.
It breeds on marshy ponds
and lakes in North and
South America.

CLASSIFICATION

ORDER ANSERIFORMES
2 FAMILIES • 51 GENERA
C. 160 SPECIES • FAMILY ANATIDAE

Characteristics Pochards look
very similar overall to dabbling
ducks. The stifftails are dumpier,
and are easily recognized by their
tail, which the drakes
often cock jauntily
up into the air. Many
species, such as the ruddy duck,
winter on coastal lagoons and
bays. Some species of pochards,
such as the greater scaup *Aythya
marila,* form up in huge rafts,
principally at sea. Both types are
birds of deep water.

Feeding Most pochards feed
chiefly on aquatic plants; scaups
dive for shellfish. Stifftails are
essentially vegetarian, although the
musk duck *Biziura lobata,* a large
Australian species, is carnivorous,
catching water beetles, crustaceans
and mollusks.

Reproduction Both types of
ducks need swamps, marshes,
lakes or other stretches of water
that have reed beds or other
vegetation that can be used for
nesting. Nests consist of a mound
of reeds or a scraped hollow in the
ground lined with grass and down.

SEA DUCKS

The sea ducks, which include scoters, goldeneyes, buffleheads and mergansers, are among the most accomplished of divers in the Anatidae family. They spend considerable time at sea, although most nest near fresh water. Three common species are the common scoter *Melanitta nigra*, the bufflehead *Bucephala albeola* and the common goldeneye *B. clangula*.

COMPANIONS IN FLIGHT
Two common scoters lead a pair of velvet scoters *Melanitta fusca*. The two species are often found together.

Characteristics The male common scoter is medium-sized with black plumage; the female is brown with gray-white checks. The bufflehead is smaller and looks somewhat tubby. The common goldeneye is often seen with the bufflehead. It is 17 to 20 inches (43–51 cm) long; the male has a large round white spot in front of his eyes.

Reproduction The common scoter breeds on the ground, along the coast in wooded areas. The bufflehead and goldeneye uses tree holes.

Habitat Most birds winter in sea bays and estuaries, and nest near freshwater lakes and ponds. With the exception of the Brazilian merganser *Mergus octosetaceus*, all sea ducks inhabit the Arctic and temperate regions of the Northern Hemisphere.

CLASSIFICATION

ORDER ANSERIFORMES
2 FAMILIES • 51 GENERA
c. 160 SPECIES • FAMILY ANATIDAE

EIDERS

The four species of eiders are specialized diving ducks, all of which inhabit coastal waters and estuaries in the Arctic and subarctic. The famous eider down is thick and heavy, with the best thermal quality of any natural substance; in some regions, such as Iceland, eiders are still farmed for their down.

The male of the king eider Somateria spectabilis has eye-catching plumage.

Characteristics Three of the eider species are extremely heavy-bodied birds, but are strong fliers nonetheless. Eider drakes in nuptial plumage are among the fanciest of ducks, although the female plumage is a well-camouflaged brown. Much of these birds' time is spent at sea, frequently in rough waters.

Feeding Eiders eat aquatic vegetation and large quantities of mollusks, sea urchins, crabs and other crustaceans. Common eiders *Somateria mollissima* prefer shellfish, such as cockles and mussels, and sea stars.

Reproduction Common eiders build down-lined nests under bushes or in crevices. Creches of several broods can form.

CLASSIFICATION

ORDER ANSERIFORMES
2 FAMILIES • 51 GENERA
c. 160 SPECIES • FAMILY ANATIDAE

SCREAMERS

The three species of South American screamers bear no superficial resemblance to typical waterfowl but are apparently closely related through a number of anatomical similarities. They are excellent swimmers and also strong fliers, able to soar for hours. They are named for their loud calls, which can be heard for long distances.

Characteristics Screamers are large, heavy-bodied birds with small heads and long legs. Their very long toes exhibit very little webbing; the long toes increase the surface area of the foot, distributing the weight and allowing them to walk over

NORTHERN SCREAMER
The northern screamer *Chauna chavaria* is one of three species of screamers that make up the Anhimidae family. All are restricted to South America.

floating vegetation. The bill is distinctly fowl-like, and each wing is armed with two long, sharp, bony spurs. The largest species, the horned screamer *Anhina cornuta*, has a peculiar frontal horn that curves forward from the forehead toward the bill.

Reproduction Screamers collect rushes and grasses from which to build shallow, cup-shaped nests on marshy ground.

Habitat Screamers are birds of marshes and wet grasslands.

CLASSIFICATION

ORDER ANSERIFORMES
2 FAMILIES • 51 GENERA
c. 160 SPECIES • FAMILY ANHIMIDAE

88

SEABIRDS AND SHOREBIRDS

The waters of the world—pools, puddles, lakes, rivers, seas and oceans—are rich in life, and are therefore valuable habitats for birds. The seabirds are beautifully adapted to roam the oceans and offshore areas, looking for fish and invertebrates. They include birds in the order Procellariiformes (the albatrosses and petrels) and those in the large order Pelecaniformes, to which the cormorants, tropicbirds and gannets belong, as well as the familiar pelicans. The shorebirds of the diverse order Charadriiformes live for the most part near the shallow waters of wetlands, beaches and tidal mudflats, although some, such as the auks, have moved out to exploit the deeper seas.

ALBATROSSES

Albatrosses (family Diomedeidae) are part of the order
Procellariiformes, birds that are highly adapted to a
marine way of life, spending much of their time at sea.
They have vast ranges. Satellite tracking studies have
shown that the wandering albatross *Diomedea
exulans* covers between 2,200 and 9,300 miles
(3,600–15,000 km), flying at speeds of up to
50 miles (80 km) per hour in a single trip.

**GRAY-HEADED
ALBATROSS**
The gray-headed
albatross *Diomedea
chrysostoma* spends
most of the year at
sea. It belongs to the
mollymawks, one of
the three groups of
albatrosses.

STORM PETRELS
Ocean birds Storm petrels are
small birds and are found in all oceans.
Many species have striking black
plumage with a white rump, and all
are colonial and nest underground,
mostly on isolated islands.

Two groups The northern group
of storm petrels have pointed wings
and short legs. They swoop down and
pluck food from the surface of the
sea. The southern group have short,
rounded wings and long legs.

Characteristics Albatrosses
are large birds, with wingspans
ranging in size from 7 feet (2.2m)
to 10 feet (3 m). The long, narrow
wings make them the supreme
exponents of gliding flight, and
they can glide for hours without a
single wing beat. There are three
groups: the great albatrosses,
which includes the wandering
albatross, and the smaller mollymawks and sooty albatrosses.
Albatrosses are distinguished from
the other Procellariiformes by the

ORDER PROCELLARIIFORMES
Birds of this order, which includes the albatrosses, fulmars and shearwaters, range the world's oceans.

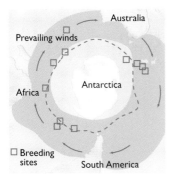

Australia

Prevailing winds

Africa

Antarctica

☐ Breeding sites

South America

CIRCLING THE POLE
The map shows the breeding sites of the wandering albatross and its movements between breeding seasons.

position of their tubular nostrils, which lie at either side of the base of the bill, rather than being fused on the top of the bill. They have an average life span of 30 years.

Feeding They eat a variety of food, often scavenging behind ships, but fish, crustaceans and squid are favorite items and are frequently caught at night. They catch prey mainly from the surface of the sea, but occasionally from just beneath the water by plunge-diving with bent wings.

Reproduction Most species breed in closely packed colonies, sometimes numbering thousands of pairs. For several species the nest is a heap of soil or vegetation,

although the tropical species make do with a scanty nest. Albatrosses usually pair for life, and they have impressive courtship displays.

Habitat Albatrosses are typically associated with the belt of windswept ocean lying between the Antarctic and the southern extremities of America, Africa and Australia, but they also breed in the more temperate waters of the Southern Hemisphere. Three species breed in the North Pacific, and one species breeds at the Galapagos Islands on the equator.

FULMARS

Fulmars make up one of the groups that comprise the diverse family of shearwaters. They are cold-water birds, only venturing into the subtropics along cold-water currents. Although similar to large gulls, with their gray-and-white plumage, fulmars are, in fact, very different.

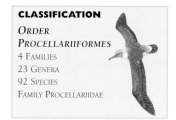

CLASSIFICATION

ORDER
PROCELLARIIFORMES
4 FAMILIES
23 GENERA
92 SPECIES
FAMILY PROCELLARIIDAE

Fulmars are expert scavengers and often congregate around fishing boats for offal.

Characteristics Fulmars are medium-sized birds with large, stout bills and a stocky build. Of the seven species, six are confined to the Southern Hemisphere. The single northern representative is the northern fulmar *Fulmaris glacialis*. Their flight is a series of fast wing beats interspersed by effortless low and fast skimming and shearing.

Feeding They feed on zooplankton and fish; most are also scavengers and are common around fishing vessels, where they feed on discarded fish and fish remains.

Reproduction Fulmars use stones or plant material to make nests on cliff ledges. If a breeding bird is approached too closely, it will spit an oily substance at the intruder.

SHEARWATERS

The shearwaters are the most diverse family of the Procellariiformes. They vary greatly in size, but typical members are about the size of small gulls. They get their name from some species' habit of skimming just over the surface of the sea. They comprise the fulmars, prions, gadfly petrels and true shearwaters. The true shearwaters are discussed here.

GLIDERS
Sooty shearwaters *Puffinus griseus* are often found with Manx shearwaters *P. puffinus* (at left with white underwing). Both are graceful gliders.

Characteristics About 23 species in the genera *Procellaria*, *Calonectris* and *Puffinus* make up the true shearwaters. Wingspan ranges from 2 feet (60 cm) to 5 feet (1.5 m). Plumage is usually black, gray or brown, with white. They are widespread birds and very mobile. The four *Procellaria* species are the biggest members of the group and are largely restricted to the southern oceans. The two *Calonectris* species breed in the North Pacific, migrating south during northern winters. The genus *Puffinus* comprises about 17 species of small to medium-sized shearwaters.

Feeding Shearwaters use their long bills to seize fish or large zooplankton under water. They are highly social birds, often forming dense feeding "rafts" at sea.

Reproduction Most species nest in vast colonies of burrows which they visit at night.

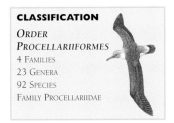

CLASSIFICATION

ORDER
PROCELLARIIFORMES
4 FAMILIES
23 GENERA
92 SPECIES
FAMILY PROCELLARIIDAE

93

A SHEARWATER'S YEAR

The life cycle of the short-tailed shearwater *Puffinus tenuirostris* includes an annual journey from its breeding islands scattered along the coasts of south and southeast Australia to reach the cool waters, but rich feeding areas, of the Bering Sea near the Alaskan coast.

JUNE/JULY/AUGUST
The birds spend their nonbreeding season in the North Pacific, arriving in in late June. Birds may go to the Arctic Ocean or the North American coast.

SEPTEMBER
Adult birds take several weeks to make the return flight south to their breeding colonies in Australia, which are usually on grassy offshore islands.

OCTOBER/NOVEMBER
After repairing their nesting burrows, courting and establishing a pair bond, the birds leave for the open sea to feed and regain condition.

Intrepid fliers The journey north and return flight south mean that these birds travel a prodigious 19,000 miles (30,000 km). The northward route stretches in an arc from Australia along the eastern rim of the Pacific. The return journey is more or less a straight line from the Bering Sea to southern Australia.

Huge numbers There are possibly 10 million breeding pairs of the short-tailed shearwater and probably an equal number of pre-breeding and nonbreeding birds. Masses of birds stream down the southeast Australian coast. Here, birders have noted as many as a quarter of a million birds passing overhead every hour.

DECEMBER/JANUARY
The egg is laid in late November and incubated by both parents in alternate shifts lasting about two weeks. The egg hatches in mid-January.

FEBRUARY/MARCH
Both parent birds bring food to the nestling chick once every three days or so in alternating visits. The chick grows quickly.

APRIL/MAY
The chick reaches its peak weight and puts on feathers. Parents and chick leave independently for their wintering grounds in the North Pacific.

PELICANS

One family in the order Pelecaniformes is particularly well known around the world—the pelicans of the family Pelecanidae. These ungainly birds, with their large feet, waddling gait, long bill and huge pouch, have attracted attention throughout recorded history.

Characteristics All seven species of these birds have the characteristic pouch, long bill and long neck. The largest species—the Australian pelican *Pelecanus conspicillatus* and the Dalmation pelican *P. crispus*—each weighs 33 pounds (15 kg) and is

BROWN PELICAN
Despite its name, the brown pelican is mainly silvery gray. Prior to nesting, the hindneck of adults becomes dark reddish or a darker reddish brown.

63 to 71 inches (160–180 cm) in length. The adults of five species are primarily white, with some black in the primary and secondary feathers. The gray or spot-billed pelican *P. philippensis* is mainly light gray, while the brown pelican *P. occidentalis* has a complicated sequence of adult annual plumages changes.

Feeding Most pelicans feed in fresh water, although all species are able to feed in salt water. The brown pelican is the only marine

CLASSIFICATION

**ORDER
PELECANIFORMES**
5 FAMILIES
7 GENERA
56 SPECIES
FAMILY PELECANIDAE

ORDER PELECANIFORMES
The order includes the pelicans, tropic-birds, gannets and boobies, cormorants and anhingas, and frigatebirds.

AMERICAN WHITES
Large congregations of American white pelicans *P. erythrorhynchos* are seen in lagoons and estuaries during winter.

species, and the only one to dive into the water to catch a meal. The other species all feed as they sit on the surface, dipping down into the water with their bill and pouch. Groups of pelicans will herd fish into shallow water, where they are more easily caught.

Reproduction Pelicans nest in colonies, which range in size from as few as five pairs to several thousand. Males pick a nest site in the colony where they display by posturing, mainly with the head and neck, as females fly over. Once mated, the male brings nest

material to the female, who builds the nest. Adults regurgitate meals to feed the chicks.

Habitat All but the brown pelican, which is marine in its habits, are found on inland waters, estuaries and lagoons.

CORMORANTS AND ANHINGAS

These members of the order Pelecaniformes are superbly adapted for diving under water in pursuit of fish: Their feathers lack waterproofing, allowing deeper diving; they are streamlined for fast swimming; and their legs and feet, placed far back on the body, make great propellers.

DRYING TIME
Cormorants lack any waterproofing agent in their plumage, which means they have to spend part of the day drying their feathers.

Characteristics Most species of cormorants and anhingas are black and may have an iridescent green or blue sheen, while others have striking white markings. There are 28 species of cormorants (also known as shags) and 4 species of anhingas (or darters). Cormorants have long bills that are distinctly hooked at the tip. Anhingas resemble cormorants, but have longer necks, longer tails and pointed, spearlike bills. One member of the family, the

Galapagos cormorant *Nannopterum harrisi*, cannot fly. It hops in and out of the water, and nests on predator-free islands.

Feeding Their diet is mostly fish, but includes smaller amounts of squid, crustaceans, frogs, tadpoles and insect larvae.

WHITE-BREASTED CORMORANT

The white-breasted cormorant *Phalacrocorax carbo* is found in tropical Africa.

CLASSIFICATION

ORDER
PELECANIFORMES
5 FAMILIES
7 GENERA
56 SPECIES
FAMILY
PHALARCROCORACIDAE

Reproduction Tree-nesting species construct nests of twigs, whereas species that nest on rock islands or cliff ledges use seaweed, or even excreta (guano) and old bones, to build their nests. Cormorants form some of the largest and densest seabird colonies in the world. In some regions, the large quantities of guanao they produce are mined for fertilizer.

Habitat These birds are found on sea coasts and large lakes and rivers. Most live in tropical and temperate areas, but some inhabit colder Antarctic and Arctic waters. Some species are solely freshwater, others solely marine, and some are found in both habitats.

GANNETS AND BOOBIES

It is thought that the name booby is derived from the Spanish word *bobo*, which means clown or stupid fellow—probably on the basis of the bird's rather comical courtship displays. There is nothing comical, however, about the diving abilities of boobies and their cousins, the gannets. They dive like missiles, often from amazing heights, into the sea in search of their prey.

Characteristics Most boobies and gannets have a white head, neck and underside, and are white with varying degrees of brown or black on the back. Colors of the soft parts of the bill and feet vary from sky-blue in the blue-footed booby *Sula nebouxii* to vivid red in the red-footed booby *S. sula*. The body is torpedo-shaped to aid plunge-diving, and the bill has a serrated edge. Male gannets are larger than females, but the reverse is true for boobies.

NORTHERN GANNETS
The northern gannet is renowned for its dives, from heights of up to 100 feet (30 m), into the sea to catch fish.

Feeding Gannets and boobies dive into the water to capture fish and squid, feeding alone or in flocks. Sometimes gannets may even pursue fish under water, moving with powerful feet and half-opened wings. A few boobies are reported to be kleptoparasitic, chasing other boobies until they regurgitate, then stealing the meal.

Reproduction Courtship can involve much parading around, lifting of the head up high, mutual preening, fencing with bills, and tossing of heads. When seen, it does make the booby's name seem appropriate. Only Abbott's *Papasula abbotti* and red-footed boobies nest in trees, building a nest of twigs which may be lined with leafy vegetation. The others lay their egg(s) on bare ground or build a nest of twigs, debris or dirt.

Habitat The three species of gannets live primarily in temperate regions, while the six species of boobies range throughout the world's tropical and subtropical regions.

Well-known species Northern gannets *Morus bassanus* inhabit the east and west coasts of the North Atlantic. At about 34 to 40 inches (87–100 cm) in length, they are among the largest seabirds. They breed on rocky islands in large colonies. The adults are white with a yellowish head and large black wing tips. The juveniles are brown, with many small white spots. In the course of five years, the birds gain adult plumage, slowly getting whiter as the molt progresses. Large feeding flocks often comprise birds in all plumage stages, from almost entirely juvenile to fully adult.

The blue-footed booby is restricted to the eastern Pacific Ocean.

CLASSIFICATION

ORDER
PELECANIFORMES
5 FAMILIES
7 GENERA
56 SPECIES
FAMILY SULIDAE

FRIGATEBIRDS

The five species of frigatebird range widely over tropical oceans during the non-nesting season and nest on isolated islands. With their huge wing area—wingspan is up to 8 feet (2.5 m)—and light weight, they have the lowest wing-loading of any bird measured and can remain in the air for days, feeding on the wing.

Characteristics All species look similar: Males are mostly black with a large red gular sac, and females are mostly dark brown.

RED DISPLAY
A male frigatebird inflates his red pouch as part of a display aimed at coaxing a female flying overhead to land beside him.

CLASSIFICATION

ORDER
PELECANIFORMES
5 FAMILIES
7 GENERA
56 SPECIES
FAMILY FREGATIDAE

Feeding They grab fish or squid from near the surface of the water or catch flying fish. They also chase and harass other birds, causing them to regurgitate and then stealing the meal.

Reproduction Males display in groups to passing females by presenting the inflated red sac, fluttering the wings, bill clattering and whinnying. After pairing, a single egg is laid in a nest of twigs.

TROPICBIRDS

Tropicbirds are characterized by a pair of slender tail streamers, which may be equal in length to the rest of the body. Except when breeding, they are solitary inhabitants of the open oceans, spending most of their lives on the wing. Amazingly, they cannot walk—their legs are located too far back on the body—and to move on land they push forward with both feet and plop on the belly.

WHITE-TAILED TROPICBIRD
White-tailed tropicbirds *Phaethon lepturus* inhabit tropical and subtropical seas around the world. They spend most of their time in the air.

Characteristics The three species (genus *Phaethon*) are similar in appearance, being white with some black on the head, back and primaries. They all have two long central tail feathers.

Feeding They are plunge-divers, diving into the water from varying heights to catch fish or squid.

Reproduction Tropicbirds perform their courtship rituals in the air, flying around in groups of two to twelve or more, squawking loudly. A pair will land and push their way into the potential nest site, a hole in a cliff or under a bush, where they sit and squawk at each other, somehow deciding whether or not to form a pair.

Habitat Widely distributed in tropical and subtropical seas, they occur in the Caribbean, Atlantic, Pacific and Indian Oceans, and are not seen on land during the nonbreeding season.

CLASSIFICATION

ORDER
PELECANIFORMES
5 FAMILIES
7 GENERA
56 SPECIES
FAMILY PHAETHONTIDAE

CURLEWS AND SANDPIPERS

The family Scolopacidae includes 88 species of birds that mostly inhabit seashores, especially tidal mudflats. Most are gregarious and habitually congregate in large mixed roosting flocks at high tide, scattering to feed over exposed mudflats as the tide recedes. The family is part of the large and diverse order Charadriiformes, the waders and shorebirds.

CLASSIFICATION

ORDER
CHARADRIIFORMES
14 FAMILIES
82 GENERA
292 SPECIES
FAMILY SCOLOPACIDAE

LONG-BILLED CURLEW
The plumage of the long-billed curlew *Numenius americanus* blends well with its grassy surroundings as it sits at its nest. It nests in grasslands and marshes in the interior west of the United States.

Characteristics Curlews and sandpipers tend to have cryptically colored, brown or grayish, streaked plumage, but may assume brighter orange or black patterns when breeding. They share a similar structure—a long body, narrow wings and long legs—but in size they vary from the eastern curlew *Numenius madagascariensis* at about 26 inches (66 cm) to the least sandpiper *Calidris minutilla* at 4½ inches (11–12 cm). Most bills are narrow, varying in length and curvature. Snipe and woodcock have proportionately the longest bills, and probe deep into the soft mud of inland marshes.

Feeding The bills of most of these birds seem designed to exploit part of the range of organisms in the mud and sand of the birds' winter quarters. The long downward-curving bills of curlews, for example, probe into worm burrows in mud, while the long straight ones of godwits search mud under water. The bills of sandpipers and curlews have sensory nerve endings near the tip, enabling the birds to sense food as they probe blindly. On rich mudflats, large flocks of these birds can feed together.

Reproduction Aerial displays are accompanied by the musical piping calls typical of these birds.

The eggs, usually three or four, are often laid in bare scrapes. The downy young usually feed themselves from the earliest stage.

Habitat Most members of the family Scolopacidae breed in the Northern Hemisphere, many using the short summer of the Arctic tundra. The breeding season may be short, and when it ends the birds migrate south to other shallow waters or coasts, some, such as the sharp-tailed sandpiper *Calidris acuminata*, traveling as far as Australasia.

A lesser yellowlegs Tringa flavipes *(center) is about the size of a killdeer* Charadrius vociferus *(right), while a greater yellowlegs* T. melanoleuca *(left) is clearly bigger.*

ORDER CHARADRIIFORMES
This order includes curlews and sandpipers, oystercatchers, plovers and dotterels, gulls, terns and auks.

SPOTTED SANDPIPER

This small bird, with its brown and white plumage and white wingstripe, may look like any sandpiper, but certain characteristics make the spotted sandpiper *Actitis macularia* one of the most distinctive North American shorebirds. For one thing, it walks with a persistent bobbing action. And in flight, the bird's wing beats are stiff and shallow, so that the wings are flicked quickly and held bowed below the body.

Characteristics The bird is about 6 to 7 inches (15.5–18 cm) long. The spots for which this species is named are present only in the summer plumage. The base of the bill and the legs are yellowish to dull pinkish in winter, as opposed to bright orangey pink in nesting birds. The spotted is set apart from other small sandpipers by the fact that it does not occur in large flocks and tends to be found alone, rather than with other shorebirds.

SPOTLESS
During winter, the spotted sandpiper loses the spots for which it is named. The bird teeters and bobs almost constantly.

Reproduction Nests consist of shallow hollows in the ground.

Habitat During migration and in winter, they are found at lakes, estuaries, reservoirs and rocky coasts. They nest along rivers during summer.

CLASSIFICATION

ORDER
CHARADRIIFORMES
14 FAMILIES
82 GENERA
292 SPECIES
FAMILY SCOLOPACIDAE

OYSTERCATCHERS

The oystercatchers, family Haematopodidae, are birds of shores, estuaries and stony rivers. They are easy to identify, usually being extremely noisy and not very shy. They differ in several respects from other waders. Parent birds, for example, bring food to their chicks, and after fledging, the young remain dependent on their parents for food for some time.

OYSTERCATCHING BILL
Oystercatchers, like this Eurasian one *Haematopus ostralegus*, use their strong bill to prise shellfish from rocks.

Characteristics They are heavy in build, and the long bill has a blunt, flattened tip that opens shellfish and chips limpets off rocks, as well as taking other prey. The plumage is black or pied.

Feeding Individual oyster-catchers specialize in catching a specific kind of food: Some feed mainly on worms, while others catch crabs, and again others mussels or cockles. By looking closely at the shape of its bill tip, it is possible to deduce what a bird's feeding preferences are.

Reproduction In saltmarshes, oystercatchers sometimes breed close together. Here they compete for the best partner and for the best breeding site, which will be close to the mudflats where they feed. The nest is a shallow cup.

CLASSIFICATION

ORDER
CHARADRIIFORMES
14 FAMILIES
82 GENERA
292 SPECIES
FAMILY
HAEMATOPODIDAE

PLOVERS AND DOTTERELS

The 66 species of the family Charadriidae are birds of coasts and open country. They have a characteristic habit of dashing over sand or mud on twinkling feet, with head held low, then periodically coming to an abrupt halt, as though called smartly to attention.

Characteristics These birds have long, pointed wings, rather large, dark eyes and a pigeonlike bill. They are moderately long-legged, and usually show bold, bright color patterns.

Feeding They feed in a "run and snatch" fashion on visible prey, such as insects, crustaceans and other types of arthropods.

LESSER GOLDEN-PLOVER

The lesser golden-plover *Pluvialis dominica* migrates regularly from western Alaska and Siberia to as far south as Australia. It is shown here in its breeding plumage.

Reproduction They are territorial when breeding, usually with conspicuous aerial displays—the Eurasian lapwing *Vanellus vanellus* being famous for its erratic, broad-winged tumbling. Plovers with young or eggs often use injury-feigning displays to distract predators.

CLASSIFICATION

ORDER
CHARADRIIFORMES
14 FAMILIES
82 GENERA
292 SPECIES
FAMILY CHARADRIIDAE

LAPWING

The Eurasian lapwing *Vanellus vanellus* is common and widespread across Britain and Europe, and is a characteristic bird of meadows, coastal pastures and arable fields. The striking crest and glossy green back is unique among European waders.

CLASSIFICATION

**ORDER
CHARADRIIFORMES**
14 FAMILIES
82 GENERA
292 SPECIES
FAMILY CHARADRIIDAE

Both male and female lapwings have crests, but the male's (shown here) is longer.

Characteristics Lapwings are about 11 to 12 inches in length (28–30 cm). Their crests make them readily identifiable. Lapwings molt into winter plumage, which is characterized by brown edges to the feathers on the back and wings and pale edges to the throat. These fringes will wear away during winter, revealing more and more green glossy plumage as spring approaches.

Lapwing chicks crouch among the grass when they hear their parents' alarm calls.

Feeding They feed mainly on earthworms. When these become inaccessible in winter, most lapwings move south to frost-free areas.

Reproduction Lapwings prefer areas of short grass, in which they start breeding very early in spring. The male performs conspicuous display flights. Nests are shallow depressions lined with grass.

109

GOLDEN-PLOVER

The golden-plover *Pluvialis apricaria* is a handsome and common winter visitor in grasslands and coastal areas in Britain and continental Europe. In summer, it breeds in moors and bogs in northern latitudes, including Scandinavia and Iceland.

Male and female adult golden-plovers (left) share the species' distinctive spangled upper plumage in summer; juveniles (right) are much plainer.

Characteristics Golden-plovers are between 10½ and 11½ inches (27–29 cm) in length. They have a short bill and longish legs. Birds in summer plumage are golden brown above, black below, with a white band from head to vent. The autumn molt replaces the black feathers with white ones.

Feeding Their diet is made up mainly of insects, mollusks and small shellfish. Like other plovers, "goldies" feed with a distinctive stop–start action, standing still, then running and picking at the ground, then standing still again. This hyper-alert behavior is aimed mainly at foiling attempts by other birds, such as gulls, from stealing any prey they might find.

Reproduction The nest consists of a shallow depression in tundra or moorland.

CLASSIFICATION

ORDER
CHARADRIIFORMES
14 FAMILIES
82 GENERA
292 SPECIES
FAMILY CHARADRIIDAE

STILTS AND AVOCETS

These slender, long-legged, long-billed birds make up the family Recurvirostridae. They are waders, favoring the shores of shallow lakes and lagoons. Unlike other waders, they have webbed feet, which enable the birds to swim as they feed.

CLASSIFICATION

ORDER
CHARADRIIFORMES
14 FAMILIES
82 GENERA
292 SPECIES
FAMILY
RECURVIROSTRIDAE

Characteristics Stilts and avocets are characterized by their long legs and long bills. Plumage is predominantly black and white. The avocets (genus *Recurvirostra*) have pied plumage with a head varying from black and white to chestnut, buff or all-white. Their very thin, long bill is upturned.

Feeding These birds search the water surface or the surface of submerged mud for small aquatic animals. The banded stilt

Cladorhynchus leucocephalus feeds on brine shrimp in Australian salt lakes and brackish estuaries. The black-winged or pied stilt *Himantopus himantopus* wades belly-deep in water, picking food from the surface.

Reproduction
Stilts and avocets breed near water, usually in colonies.

AVOCET
The young of avocets
Recurvirostra avosetta
have the characteristic
upcurve to their bills.

GULLS

The gulls of the family Laridae are a readily recognizable group, solidly built, with long, strong web-footed legs for running and swimming, and long wings for the steady, sustained flight that goes with aerial scavenging. Their harsh cackling, squawking or wailing calls are ubiquitous sounds of the seaside.

The ring-billed gull Larus delawarensis, of North America, is often quite tame and will beg and scavenge at picnic tables and on beaches.

Characteristics With a few dusky exceptions, the plumage is mainly white with gray or black across the back and wings. There is little conspicuous patterning, but some species have a brown or black hood that combines with a red or yellow bill to act as a display pattern. Color and pattern are similar in both sexes, and young birds have mottled brown plumage with dark bills and a dark tail band.

Feeding Gulls eat a wide variety of food, including insects, carrion and small marine life exposed by tides, and will take any small creatures. The larger gulls will attack and kill young or smaller seabirds. (They are probably responsible for the nocturnal nesting habits of many smaller seabirds.) As scavengers, they have readily learnt to use discarded waste from human activity, following boats, searching recently plowed land and feeding on rubbish tips. Gulls tend to be sociable when feeding, and will respond quickly when the behavior of individuals indicates that food has been found.

Reproduction Nesting is usually colonial, using sites varying from cliff ledges to level

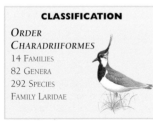

CLASSIFICATION

ORDER
CHARADRIIFORMES
14 FAMILIES
82 GENERA
292 SPECIES
FAMILY LARIDAE

ground, and from the Chilean deserts to polar shores. The small North American Bonaparte's gull *Larus philadelphia* is an exception, nesting inland in conifer trees. A gull's nest is usually a substantial cup of vegetation. The dark-mottled, downy young are fed by the adults, but are mobile and even when feathered may run and hide if threatened. On the nests of kittiwakes (*Rissa* species), which are trampled drums of mud and plants fixed to small projections of precipitous cliffs, the young are adapted to making little movement on the site.

Habitat The 48 species are spread around the shorelines and islands of the world, and to the larger inland waters. The largest number of species is found in the Pacific Ocean region.

SHRILL VOICES

Many calls and postures of gulls around the world are highly ritualized, and differ only in detail from species to species. These are kelp gulls *Larus dominicanus*, which are found in Australia, New Zealand, South Africa and southern South America.

BLACK-HEADED GULL

The black-headed gull *Larus ridibundus* is the most common and widespread gull in Europe, and is very well adapted to an urban way of life. It will take almost any type of food, and can be found outside the breeding season almost everywhere, including inner cities.

The distinctive chocolate-brown cap of the black-headed gull is replaced in the winter months by much plainer markings.

Characteristics These gulls are about 15 to 17 inches (38–44 cm) long. During summer they have a chocolate-brown cap with white "eyebrows," which accounts for the common name. In winter, the dark feathers are largely replaced by white ones, leaving a black spot on the head.

Reproduction They breed in noisy and often very large colonies. The nest is a shallow, scruffy cup of dry grass and leaves.

Habitat Black-headed gulls breed near water, usually on small islands across a large part of Britain and northern and eastern continental Europe. They are so well adapted to the human environment that they do not usually migrate over large distances. Many birds from the north and east spend the winter in Western Europe, due to the mild climate and the extensive urban areas that meet all of their feeding and roosting requirements.

CLASSIFICATION

ORDER
CHARADRIIFORMES
14 FAMILIES
82 GENERA
292 SPECIES
FAMILY LARIDAE

KITTIWAKE

Kittiwakes *Rissa tridactyla* are the most pelagic of the northwestern European gulls; they come ashore only to breed, spending the remainder of the year at sea, often far away from land. They get their common name from their rather nasal cry of *kitti-wake*.

CLASSIFICATION

ORDER
CHARADRIIFORMES
14 FAMILIES
82 GENERA
292 SPECIES
FAMILY LARIDAE

Characteristics They are about 16 to 17 inches (40–44 cm) long, with short black legs. The upper parts are pale gray and the wing tips uniformly black without the white "mirrors" of the common gull *Larus canus*.

Feeding The birds feed at sea most of the year, taking fish from the surface or offal from trawlers.

Reproduction Kittiwakes breed on ledges of steep cliffs. The young do not fall off the ledges because, unlike other gull chicks, they instinctively face away from steep drops.

PLUMAGE CHANGE
In flight, the juvenile kittiwake (right) has a black trim on the upper wings. The adult (left) has black only on the wing tips.

Kittiwakes nest in close-packed colonies on precipitous cliff ledges.

TERNS

Terns are members of the same family as gulls, the
Laridae, and they look similar. But, with their more
slender build, longer, more pointed wings and
forked tails, they are adapted for a more specialized
type of feeding—plunge-diving into the sea.

TWIN TERNS
The black bill tip of the common tern
Sterna hirundo (the two birds at right)
sets it apart from the almost identical
arctic tern *S. paradisaea.*

SKUAS

Scavengers Skuas or jaegers (family
Stercorariidae) consist of seven gull-
like species, but are brown in color
with white wing patches. The largest
species (genus *Catharacta*) breed on
shores of cold seas. They scavenge
around seabird colonies, taking eggs
and young, and killing weak birds.

Thieves Smaller skuas (genus
Stercorarius) breed on the Arctic
tundra. They steal other birds' meals
and also kill small mammals and birds.

Characteristics

Plumage tends to be
pale gray and white, with
black on the crown or nape, but a
few species are mainly brown or
black. The wings are long and
slender, the tail distinctly forked,
the bill strong, thin and tapering,
and the legs small and short, with
webbed feet. The sea terns range
in size from the big Caspian tern
Sterna caspia at 21 inches (53 cm)
to the little tern *S. albifrons* at
9½ inches (24 cm).

Feeding *Chlidonias* species, the
so-called "marsh terns," feed

ROYAL TERNS

The royal tern *Sterna maxima* breeds in coastal Central America and west Africa. The distinctive black cap is partly replaced in winter by a large white forehead patch.

CLASSIFICATION

ORDER
CHARADRIIFORMES
14 FAMILIES
82 GENERA
292 SPECIES
FAMILY LARIDAE

Reproduction Sea terns are highly sociable nesters, making a collection of scrapes, unlined unless material is to hand, on beaches, sandbanks and low, sparsely vegetated shores. Birds nesting on hot tropical beaches may shade the nest at times, and may moisten eggs or chicks with wet belly feathers.

mainly by briefly dipping to snatch tiny creatures from the surface of inland waters; they also hunt insects over land. The sea terns fly low over oceanic or inland waters, spotting prey, hovering briefly, and then plunging for their quarry, often sending up a plume of spray as they hit the water.

ARCTIC TERN

The arctic tern *Sterna paradisaea* is a handsome, black-capped bird with a wide distribution. Its seasonal migrations are truly remarkable: From its Arctic breeding grounds, it crosses the equator to spend the nonbreeding season in the pack-ice fringing the Antarctic continent.

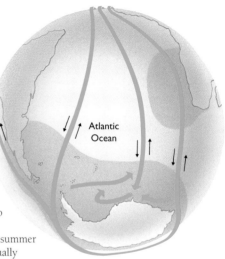

Characteristics The arctic tern is approximately 15 to 17 inches (38–43 cm) long, with a rather short coral-red bill. The upper parts are gray and there is a narrow black line on the under-wing; all flight feathers are translucent when viewed from below. The legs are short. The species is especially noted for its long seasonal migrations. It breeds between May and August on the frigid shores of the Arctic Ocean, then migrates to the fringes of Antarctica, on the opposite side of the world, where it spends the period November to March. In doing so, it passes from a northern summer to a southern one, annually accumulating some of the longest day lengths of any bird. The young migrate independently of their parents, and typically spend up to four years in the Southern Ocean before returning north to breed for the first time.

EPIC JOURNEY
The arctic tern has the longest migration route of any bird—some 12,400 miles (20,000 km).

▉ Migration paths
▧ Wintering areas

Feeding The arctic tern is a typical sea tern, spending much of its time in the air over oceans, spotting food in the water and plunge-diving for it. Plankton, fish and crustaceans are the main food items.

Reproduction Artic terns breed in colonies on shingle beaches and among rocks north of the Arctic Circle between May and August. Displaying males parade around their mates with plumage sleeked and a small fish held high. The nest is a scrape in the bare ground, often lined with shells, vegetation or debris. The female lays two or three eggs. The nestlings are tended by both parents, who bring fish to the chicks in their bills, sometimes feeding them while still in the air. Adult Arctic terns defend their nests against predators by dive-bombing.

Arctic terns hover over water before diving for fish.

Habitat These terns have a widespread breeding distribution in high latitudes of the Northern Hemisphere, and in winter fly south to the edge of the pack-ice along the Antarctic coastline.

CLASSIFICATION

ORDER
CHARADRIIFORMES
14 FAMILIES
82 GENERA
292 SPECIES
FAMILY LARIDAE

119

CASPIAN TERN

A deep, throaty, slightly scratchy *rrah* call often draws attention to an adult Caspian tern *Sterna caspia* flying overhead. The large size—it is the largest of all terns—huge red bill and black underside of the primaries distinguish this bird from all other tern species.

Characteristics The Caspian tern is about the size of some larger gulls, and is readily identifiable by its stout, carrot-red bill, black cap and the large dark patch under each wingtip, visible when the bird is in flight.

This juvenile (right) will soon join its parents on their annual migration flight.

Reproduction Caspian terns breed along sandy or rocky coasts. Their nests are shallow scrapes on the ground.

Habitat The species has a very wide distribution, and breeds on all continents except South America and Antarctica.

SKIMMERS

The skimmers (genus *Rynchops*) are superficially ternlike birds, but they are set apart by their extraordinary bill, in which the lower mandible is flattened and is much longer than the rounded upper mandible. The bill is an essential part of the feeding method, which gives these birds their common name.

Characteristics Skimmers are white with black wings and crown. Relying wholly on flight for feeding, and resting on the sandbars or gravel of shores and rivers at other times, they have long, tapering wings, short tails with a fork, and shortish legs with webbed feet. The flight is light and graceful with steady, shallow beats of raised wings. The highly asymmetrical bill is their most obvious feature.

Feeding They usually feed by skimming low over the water with the tip of the longer, lower mandible plowing a little below the surface. When prey is touched, it is snapped up.

Habitat Skimmers are birds of coasts and rivers. There is one species each in Africa, India and the Americas.

BLACK SKIMMER
The black skimmer *Rynchops niger* inhabits coasts and rivers in North, Central and South America, and in the Caribbean.

CLASSIFICATION

ORDER
CHARADRIIFORMES
14 FAMILIES
82 GENERA
292 SPECIES
FAMILY LARIDAE

AUKS

The auks (family Alcidae) are short-winged marine diving birds. They look stout and stubby when floating or paddling at the surface, but under water they are more streamlined and move with agility, swimming with strong strokes of the wings and steering with the feet.

CLASSIFICATION

ORDER
CHARADRIIFORMES
14 FAMILIES
82 GENERA
292 SPECIES
FAMILY ALCIDAE

Characteristics Auks have largish heads and thick, waterproof plumage on a compact body. The wings are short, small, strong and firm-feathered for swimming. Plumage is largely black above and white beneath. Flight is usually direct and low over the water. Having small tails, they tend to use their splayed, webbed feet in maneuvering. The bill shape varies considerably. The guillemots, or murres, birds of colder and Arctic seas, have narrow, tapering bills.

GREAT AUK
Largest of the alcids, the great auk weighed 11 pounds (5 kg). It was killed for its flesh, and the last birds died in 1844.

Puffins (*Fratercula* species) have stout, deep bills with serrated edges, in which they can carry a considerable quantity of food for their young. The little auk *Alle alle* is a tiny bird with a big head and stubby bill. In the North Pacific, the smallest members of the auk family are known as murrelets and auklets

Feeding The larger species take mostly fish, but the smaller ones may rely on plankton. Shellfish and worms are also eaten.

PUFFIN
During the breeding season, the bill of the male Atlantic puffin *Fratercula arctica* develops bright colors, a contrast to its plain plumage.

GUILLEMOTS
The guillemots, or murres, are larger auks up to about 18 inches (46 cm) long. They have long, pointed bills, and breed on rocky coasts in far northern latitudes. Outside the breeding season, the common guillemot *Uria aalgae* (above left) stays at sea, far away from the coast. The similar but much smaller black guillemot *Cepphus grylle* (above right) always stays closer to the coast. Like all but the smallest auks, their main food is fish.

Reproduction Auks usually breed in colonies on ledges or in crevices on rocky coasts or islands. Puffins burrow into the softer soil-covering of cliffs and islands, and they gather nest material. Breeding may bring vivid colors on the bill and gape of some auk species, as well as feather adornments on the head. The young of some auk species flutter down from the nesting ledge before they are fully fledged and go out to sea escorted by their parents.

Habitat Auks are birds of northern latitudes, and they are found in the open sea and coastal waters of the North Pacific, North Atlantic and Arctic Oceans.

BIRDS OF PREY

The raptors make up the main grouping of birds of prey. The Latin word raptor means "one who seizes and carries away," a term that immediately calls to mind the archetypal eagles, the most powerful of avian predators. Yet the order Falconiformes—one of the largest and most fascinating of all avian groups—includes an unexpected range of form and habit, from swift, bird-catching falcons, among the fastest of birds, to huge, ugly, carrion-eating Old World vultures. Also included in this group, for convenience, are the New World vultures, although they are not related. Raptors hunt by day; owls (order Strigiformes) and nightjars and frogmouths (order Caprimulgiformes) take the night shift.

THE WORLD OF RAPTORS

Raptors (order Falconiformes) are characterized by hooked bills, strong feet, sharply curved talons and large eyes. Typically, they hunt by day and eat live prey caught with their feet. Also characteristic is the crop (a pouchlike extension of the gullet) to store freshly eaten food.

A TALE OF TWO VULTURES

Convergent evolution The two groups of vultures are a fascinating example of convergent evolution: two quite unrelated groups of animals that look alike because they have developed the same adaptations for a similar way of life.

Old and New The 15 species of Old World vultures, living in Africa, Asia and Europe, share a common ancestry with eagles and hawks. The seven species of New World vultures are probably descended from the same line as the storks.

Types Differences in basic raptor design are adaptations to the wide variety of behavior in this order. Vultures soar on long, broad wings and have strong feet and fairly straight talons; they must search vast distances to find carrion, then hold it while they tear it with their bills. The falcons have a muscular body, long pointed wings and long

TALONS MADE FOR THE JOB

A raptor's talons match its prey. A sea eagle's (top) long talons grip fish; a brown goshawk's (center) grab small mammals; and a sparrowhawk's (bottom) catch birds.

ORDER FALCONIFORMES
Raptors can be found in almost every habitat, from Arctic tundra to equatorial rain forest; farmland to city.

POWERS OF SIGHT
All raptors, such as this red-tailed hawk *Buteo jamaicensis*, hunt by sight, and their eyes are large and their vision excellent. Some eagles have vision that is twice as acute as that of humans.

toes—all necessary for swift, agile flight and capture of airborne prey. Many of the kites have a relatively slim body and weak, fleshy feet, reflecting their generally less predatory habits and their scavenging or collecting of easy prey. Long-legged sparrowhawks and harriers reach into bushes or grass. Some of the forest eagles have massive legs and talons for capturing large mammals.

Families Three families of diurnal birds of prey are recognized: Accipitridae (hawks and eagles), Sagittariidae (the secretary bird) and Falconidae (falcons). The accipitrids form the largest group.

OSPREY

Keen birders may be lucky enough to witness the spectacular sight of an osprey *Pandion haliaetus* diving feet-first into the water, coming up with a fish and carrying it off in its talons. While today the osprey is common in many parts of the world, from the 1950s through the 1970s many populations declined drastically, mainly as a result of the misuse of pesticides.

BACK FROM THE BRINK
The increase in osprey numbers is partly due to the provision of artificial nesting platforms such as this one.

Characteristics The osprey is predominantly white below with long, gull-like wings and a rather short barred tail. The upper parts are dark brown, except for the white crown of the head. The dark stripe across the sides of the face, crossing the yellow eye, is distinctive. There is brown streaking on the upper breast, especially in immature birds. Ospreys are medium-sized raptors, about 22 inches (56 cm) in length. They utter a variety of high, yelping calls.

CLASSIFICATION

ORDER FALCONIFORMES
3 FAMILIES
76 GENERA
300 SPECIES
FAMILY ACCIPITRIDAE

Feeding The osprey catches fish by plunging into water from the air. It carries its prey in one talon with the fish's head facing forward, in order to be more streamlined for flying. Its catch may weigh up to about 7 pounds (3 kg). To secure the slippery prey, the osprey has sharply curved talons and spiny scales on the toe pads. The osprey is also known to take mammals, birds and sea snakes.

Reproduction Both sexes build the large stick-nest, which is placed on trees, rock pinnacles and manmade structures. On islands free from predators, they may even nest on the ground. The female takes the main role in incubating the two or three eggs, while she is fed by the male on fish carried to the nest.

Habitat Ospreys live along rivers, lakes and coasts that provide ice-free and relatively calm waters. They are found almost worldwide, but mainly only as a migrant in the Southern Hemisphere, except Australasia, where they breed.

FISH-KILLER
The osprey hovers over lakes and rivers to locate fish, then plunges in feet-first. When it reaches its feeding perch, it waits for its prey to die before eating it, drying itself in the meantime.

129

HOOK-BILLED KITE

The hook-billed kite *Chondrohierax uncinatus* is a small raptor that inhabits dense undergrowth in forest and woodland in tropical South America, from Mexico south to northern Argentina and Paraguay and including some islands in the West Indies. Its most readily identifiable feature is the heavy and very hooked bill, which is used to eat its preferred prey, snails.

Characteristics Adult males are most often gray above with fine white bars on the gray under parts. Adult females are usually dark brown above with a gray head, the under parts rufous with fine white bars.

Feeding They feed mainly on snails, sometimes hanging upside down by the feet while foraging in trees, and congregating in flocks of up to two dozen birds.

Reproduction A small stick-nest is built in the outer branches of a tree. Two eggs are laid.

CLASSIFICATION

ORDER FALCONIFORMES
3 FAMILIES
76 GENERA
300 SPECIES
FAMILY ACCIPITRIDAE

The bill of the hook-billed kite is designed to crush snail shells or tease out the mollusks from within.

BLACK-SHOULDERED KITE

The small, elegant form of a black-shouldered kite *Elanus caeruleus* can be seen hovering, or perched on a treetop vantage point, in most open savannas and grasslands of tropical and subtropical regions, from Spain to southern China, Indonesia and Papua New Guinea.

The eyes of the black-shouldered kite are a brilliant ruby red.

Characteristics This kite is white except for the dove-gray upper parts, crown and flight feathers; there are prominent black patches on the upper wings, from which the bird derives its name.

Feeding They eat mainly rodents, although some small birds, lizards and a few insects are also taken.

Reproduction The nest is a flimsy platform of sticks and weeds. The female may leave the family before the chicks fledge to find a new mate.

CLASSIFICATION

ORDER FALCONIFORMES
3 FAMILIES
76 GENERA
300 SPECIES
FAMILY ACCIPITRIDAE

BRAHMINY KITE

The brahminy kite *Haliastur indus* is found along shores and estuaries from India and Sri Lanka through the islands of South-East Asia to the northern coast of Australia. Its white head, breast and neck and chestnut upper parts make this one of the most handsome of kites.

This kite cannot kill large animals, and instead hunts small prey, such as fish and frogs, which are often taken as carrion.

Characteristics The brahminy kite is a medium-sized raptor, about 17 inches (43 cm) long. The white head, neck and upper breast contrast sharply with the rich chestnut color of the remainder of the plumage. The eyes are dark brown. It utters mewing and wailing calls.

CLASSIFICATION

ORDER FALCONIFORMES

3 FAMILIES
76 GENERA
300 SPECIES
FAMILY ACCIPITRIDAE

Feeding These birds feed mainly on small vertebrates, including many fish, and much of it is taken as carrion.

Reproduction A pair builds a substantial stick-nest over a fork within the foliage of a tall tree. One or two eggs are laid.

WHITE-BELLIED SEA EAGLE

With a wingspan of 6½ feet (2 m), the white-bellied sea eagle *Haliaeetus leucogaster* is a striking raptor of coasts, estuaries and large rivers from India and Sri Lanka, through South-East Asia and Indonesia to New Guinea and Australia.

The white-belled sea eagle can snatch fish from the water with one sweep of its huge talons.

Characteristics This eagle is about 32 inches (80 cm) long, and is white except for the blue-gray upper parts and black flight feathers. There is a broad white band at the tip of the short tail. It utters braying cries and yelps.

Feeding White-bellied sea eagles catch fish, sea snakes and water birds. They also eat carrion, and rob other birds of their prey.

Reproduction The nest is a huge structure of sticks placed in a tree or on a cliff.

CLASSIFICATION

ORDER FALCONIFORMES
3 FAMILIES
76 GENERA
300 SPECIES
FAMILY ACCIPITRIDAE

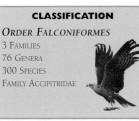

BLACK KITE

The black kite *Milvus migrans* is a medium-sized raptor with a wide distribution from southern Europe, through much of Africa and Asia, to Australia. The common name is somewhat misleading—the bird is brown rather than black.

Characteristics Black kites have dark brown upper parts and more rufous under parts; all feathers are streaked in the center with black. The long wing feathers and deeply forked tail are dark brown barred with lighter brown, and the forehead and face are washed with pale gray in some forms. The eyes may be dark brown or cream and the bill yellow or black, according to which population the individual belongs to. Immature birds are similar to adults, but have the under parts streaked with pale brown, the upper parts tipped with rufous and the tail less deeply forked. Adults are about 22 inches (55 cm) in length.

Feeding The black kite is a most catholic feeder, dextrous in flight at catching small animals or scavenging scraps. It will readily take carrion, including fish, and eats some snails and palm nuts when available.

RED KITE

A close relative of the black kite is the red kite *Milvus milvus,* one of the most elegant and handsome raptors in Europe. The bird has largely rusty-red body plumage and a gray head. Apart from coloration, the main points of difference compared to the black kite are the larger size of the red kite and its longer, more obviously forked tail. This is a true continental European endemic bird species, with an isolated population in Wales. It has been heavily persecuted in the past and decisive action has been taken to protect the species, including recent reintroduction programs in parts of England and Scotland. It lives on small rodents and birds and large insects, but also takes carrion.

Reproduction Prior to nesting, mates pursue one another in skilful weaving flights and utter mewing calls. Both sexes build the flimsy stick platform in the fork of a tree, and two or three eggs, varying in size within clutches, are laid on a lining of rubbish and debris. The female does most of the 29 to 35 days of incubation, fed by the male but also gathering her own food. The nestling period lasts about six weeks, and the female is most attentive to the chicks during the early stages.

Habitat Open woodland is preferred, but black kites will occupy habitats ranging from forest to desert if food is available.

The black kite is adept at scooping live fish from water, but carrion also makes up a significant proportion of its diet.

CLASSIFICATION

ORDER FALCONIFORMES
3 FAMILIES
76 GENERA
300 SPECIES
FAMILY ACCIPITRIDAE

135

SWALLOW-TAILED KITE

This unusual-looking raptor inhabits forests, grasslands and savanna from the southeastern United States down to southern Argentina. The swallow-tailed kite *Elanoides forficatus* earns its common name not only from the shape of the tail but also from its habit of drinking in flight by dipping low over water, like a swallow.

With its black-and-white plumage and long, deeply forked tail, the swallow-tailed kite is unlikely to be mistaken for any other species.

Characteristics The snowy white head and under parts of the swallow-tailed kite make a striking contrast with its glossy black upper parts and flight feathers. The wings are slender and the tail elongated and forked. It is about 24 inches (60 cm) long.

Feeding Insects and tree frogs, taken in the air or from foliage, make up the main part of the diet. Eggs, nestlings, reptiles and fruit are also taken.

Reproduction Dramatic aerial maneuvers are a prelude to nesting. Several nests are placed close to one another, high up in trees. The female does most of the incubation of the two to four eggs, and later helps the male to feed the chicks.

CLASSIFICATION

ORDER FALCONIFORMES
3 FAMILIES
76 GENERA
300 SPECIES
FAMILY ACCIPITRIDAE

BATELEUR

The bateleur *Terathopius ecaudatus* is a large and handsome eagle found throughout Africa south of the Sahara and into Arabia. Its wings, like those of a modern glider, are unusually long and narrow, enabling it to swiftly cover large amounts of territory in search of food.

CLASSIFICATION

ORDER FALCONIFORMES
3 FAMILIES
76 GENERA
300 SPECIES
FAMILY ACCIPITRIDAE

short tail and upturned wingtips create a distinctive shape in flight. It is about 24 inches (60 cm) long.

Feeding Being birds of the African savanna, they take a wide range of prey, including birds, reptiles, and mammals from antelopes to mice.

Characteristics This is a colorful bird, with a crimson face and plumage that is a combination of black, gray and rufous. The

Reproduction The bateleur is known for its spectacular courtship flights. A single egg is laid in a large stick-nest.

This bird's common name is French for "tightrope-walker," a reference to its gliding pattern of flight, in which it continually tilts from side to side.

137

OLD WORLD VULTURES

Old World vultures are members of the Accipitridae, the same family as hawks and eagles. Vultures are scavengers that rarely kill prey. They are incapable of sustained flapping flight and depend on rising air currents to keep them aloft. Because of the vast distances they can travel in search of carcasses, they are exceptionally efficient and important scavengers.

Characteristics Because of their dependence on soaring flight, vultures have very long, wide wings. Most species have bare areas of skin on their head and neck, thought to reduce fouling of feathers when feeding and perhaps to help with heat regulation. There is also a ruff of feathers or down around the neck. Some species are brightly colored around the head.

Feeding These birds are often the main scavengers in the regions they inhabit. Species vary widely in size, and between them they can deal quickly and efficiently with most carcasses. Large species, such as the Himalayan griffon *Gyps himalayensis*, weigh up to about 22 pounds (10 kg) and feed on muscle and viscera from large carcasses; medium-sized ones weigh between 9 and 13 pounds

BEARDED VULTURE
Also called the lammergeier, the bearded vulture is huge, with a wingspan of 8 feet (2.5 m). It lives in Africa, and southern Europe east to China.

Vultures make short work of large mammal carcasses, such as this gnu's.

(4–6 kg) and take the skin, tendons, sinews and other tough tissues; the small species, which weigh just 2 to 4 pounds (1–2 kg), specialize in eating small scraps left behind by the other birds. The Egyptian vulture *Neophron percnopterus* cracks eggs and eats their contents; it picks up stones and hurls them at eggs too large to pick up and drop. The bearded vulture *Gypaetus barbatus* breaks open bones by dropping them repeatedly from a height and then extracts the marrow with its scooplike tongue.

Reproduction Like their fellow accipitrids, vultures perform aerobatic courtship displays. Nests are generally made of sticks and placed in trees or on cliff ledges. One or two eggs are laid.

Habitat These birds are found in a variety of habitats, including deserts, mountains, open plains and farmland, in Africa, southern Europe, the Middle East and Asia.

CLASSIFICATION

ORDER FALCONIFORMES
3 FAMILIES
76 GENERA
300 SPECIES
FAMILY ACCIPITRIDAE

NEW WORLD VULTURES

Seven species belong to the family Cathartidae. This group from the Americas looks remarkably like the Old World vultures, which are true birds of prey. The New World vultures are distinguished by their perforate nostrils (open from one side of the head through to the other) and their lack of a functional hind toe.

TURKEY VULTURE
The turkey vulture is common in the Americas. Adults have naked reddish heads, while juvenile birds have naked gray heads.

Characteristics New World vultures have rather dull plumage but an often colorful bare head and neck in adulthood. Corrugated, wattled skin in brilliant red, orange and yellow adorns the head of the king vulture *Sarcorhamphus papa*. Inflatable neck pouches highlight the pink-yellow bare skin during courtship displays by the California condor *Gymnogyps californianus*, and the red skin on the face and neck of the turkey vulture *Cathartes aura* becomes brighter during conflict.

Feeding All New World vultures are scavengers; turkey vultures also take a few live prey such as young birds and turtles. The three members of the genus *Cathartes* have a keen sense of smell, which they use to locate carcasses, rejecting those that are decayed. All species can go for weeks without food, then gorge when they find it.

140

BLACK VULTURE
On the ground, the American black vulture runs with a gamboling gait as it feeds at garbage dumps and wharves in the southeastern United States.

FAMILY CATHARTIDAE
The cathartids, or New World vultures, are wholly confined to North, Central and South America.

Reproduction They do not build a nest, but lay one or two eggs on the ground or on a cliff ledge, or in a tree stump or cave. Both parents care for the young and regurgitate food to feed them.

Habitat They occupy a wide range of habitats. Some, such as the American black vulture *Coragys atratus*, are closely associated with humans, often feeding at garbage dumps.

TAKE-OFF
To spot likely sources of food, vultures use their long, wide wings to glide and soar for long periods, often at great heights. Shown here is a turkey vulture.

AFRICAN HARRIER HAWK

The African harrier hawk or gymnogene *Polyboroides typus* is a bird of woodland and savanna in sub-Saharan Africa. It has a distinctive method of finding food—using its flexible legs to extract prey from awkward hollows.

CLASSIFICATION

ORDER FALCONIFORMES
3 FAMILIES
76 GENERA
300 SPECIES
FAMILY ACCIPITRIDAE

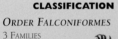

The African harrier hawk has a long tail and distinctive black spots on its back.

Characteristics The African harrier hawk is about 22 inches (55 cm) in length; the female is slightly larger than the male. It is mostly gray, with fine white bars on the breast and underwing coverts, black spots on the back, black ends to the flight feathers, and a black tail with a white bar across the center.

Feeding The bird uses its long, double-jointed legs or bare-faced head to grope in tree hollows and caves for small animals, especially nestlings, bats and squirrels. It also slowly floats past vegetation in search of prey, including insects and lizards.

Reproduction Both sexes construct the large stick-nest in a tree or, less often, on a rock ledge. One or two eggs are laid. The first chick to hatch may attack its sibling, which often succumbs.

ROUGH-LEGGED HAWK

The rough-legged hawk *Buteo lagopus* is a breeding bird of the northern tundra of North America, Europe and Asia, but winters at more southern latitudes. Much of its hunting is done on the wing, often by hovering.

The rough-legged hawk has a wingspan of about 5 feet (1.5 m).

Characteristics This large raptor has very variable plumage. It is generally dark brown above and lighter below, variously streaked with darker brown on the head, breast and thighs, and mottled with white on the back and upper wing coverts.

Feeding Lemmings are the staple food, their abundance determining the success and productivity of nesting attempts. Rodents are also the staple food outside the breeding season.

Reproduction A stick-nest is built on a rock ledge, or in a tree if available. Up to seven eggs are laid in the well-lined cup nest. Chicks leave the nest when about 40 days old, and after a further four to six weeks start their first migration.

CLASSIFICATION

ORDER FALCONIFORMES
3 FAMILIES
76 GENERA
300 SPECIES
FAMILY ACCIPITRIDAE

AMERICA'S NATIONAL EMBLEM

The bald eagle *Haliaeetus leucocephalus* is found only in North America, along coasts, rivers and large lakes. In 1782 it won the contest between it and the wild turkey to become the national bird of the United States. Chosen for its fierce demeanor, this eagle in fact tends to be timid.

Fish-hunters Bald eagles hunt mostly from perches overlooking water, plunging to catch fish with their talons before returning to a perch to eat them. The eagles also eat small birds and carrion.

High-rise nests They generally make their nests in old pine or cypress trees. For better visibility, they prefer to build as high as possible, so nests typically are 60 to 100 feet (18–30 m) off the ground. The nests themselves can be very large—the largest on

record measured 12 feet (3.6 m) from top to bottom and was estimated to weigh 4,000 pounds (1,800 kg).

Making a come-back Pesticide use and hunting led to a steep decline in bald eagle numbers. Conservation efforts have largely reversed this trend.

The bald eagle's huge talons give it a vice-like killing grip.

NOT BALD

"Bald" refers not to hairlessness but to snowy whiteness, reflecting an obsolete meaning of the word.

LOCKED IN FLIGHT

Bald eagles mate for life and maintain their pair bonds with elaborate and spectacular aerial displays before breeding each year. Part of one display involves the two birds locking talons.

GREAT PHILIPPINE EAGLE

The great Philippine eagle *Pithecohaga jefferyi* is one of the largest and most striking forest eagles in the world. But habitat loss has made it among the rarest of all raptors, with some estimates suggesting a population of less than 200 individuals, restricted to patches of rainforest on a few Philippine islands.

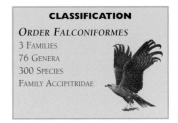

CLASSIFICATION

ORDER FALCONIFORMES
3 FAMILIES
76 GENERA
300 SPECIES
FAMILY ACCIPITRIDAE

Characteristics This superb eagle is about 38 inches (95 cm) long. The feathers of the upper parts are dark brown edged with buff. The underparts are off-white, streaked with rufous on the throat, thighs and underwing coverts. The head is surmounted by a crest of long, pale rufous feathers streaked with dark brown. The black bill is exceptionally deep and prominent. Immature birds resemble the adults, and the sexes are similar.

Feeding The great Philippine eagle is a fearsome and powerful hunter, its diet consisting mainly of arboreal mammals, such as flying lemurs and squirrels. Monkeys, deer, palm civets, bats, snakes, monitor lizards and large birds, such as hornbills, are also taken at times.

Reproduction A huge nest high in a forest tree is used over successive years, and the pair may soar in the area of the nest before breeding. Both sexes line the nest with green leaves, and a single egg is incubated, mostly by the female, for about 60 days. The male delivers food to the nest throughout the breeding cycle until assisted by the female in the latter half of the 105-day nestling period. The young only try to catch their own prey four or five months after leaving the nest. With such a prolonged cycle, successful breeding may only occur in alternate years.

Habitat The eagle lives in tropical forests on the largest Philippine islands of Luzon, Mindanao, Samar and Leyte. Populations have greatly declined because of extensive clearing of forest. The forests of the Sierra Madre mountains on Luzon represent the largest single stronghold for the species, but if deforestation continues at the present rate, the bird could soon become extinct there. The island of Samar is still well forested and could hold appreciable numbers.

MONKEY-KILLER

The great Philippine eagle hunts from a perch in a tree or patrols the forest canopy, on the lookout for flying lemurs, squirrels, large birds and monkeys.

SECRETARY BIRD

A resemblance to an early lawyer's clerk carrying a bunch of quill pens behind the ears gives the secretary bird *Sagittarius serpentarius* its common name. This unusual bird is the only living representative of the family Sagittariidae, and has no obvious close relatives.

The secretary bird's long tail and black-and-white underwings make it easy to identify in flight.

Characteristics Long, pink, storklike legs and ornamental head feathers make the secretary bird unmistakable. It has gray plumage

CLASSIFICATION

ORDER FALCONIFORMES
3 FAMILIES
76 GENERA
300 SPECIES
FAMILY SAGITTARIIDAE

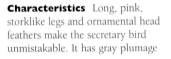

but for the black flight feathers, black tips to the crest feathers on the nape, black leggings on the thighs, and a black band across the tail. The belly and underwings are white and produce a distinctive pattern against the black flight feathers when flying with the long central tail feathers projecting. The secretary bird stands about 3 feet (1 m) tall.

Feeding The secretary bird spends much of its time on the

ground, striding about in open country. Its diet consists mainly of rodents, reptiles and locusts, which are subdued by a kick from the long legs, short stout toes and nail-like claws.

Reproduction Undulating flight displays and croaking calls are performed prior to breeding, and

a 6½-feet (2 m) diameter stick-and-weed platform on the crown of a low tree may form the nest for several successive attempts. One to three eggs are laid. The young are fed from cropfuls of prey regurgitated onto the nest floor and from a liquid trickled from the bill of the parent.

Habitat Secretary birds inhabit open woodland, steppe and grassland throughout Africa south of the Sahara.

GROUND-HUNTER
The secretary bird differs from most raptors in that it hunts from the ground, not from the air. It kills its prey, often a snake, by stomping on it.

AFRICAN PYGMY FALCON

The largest falcons are powerful birds, capable of swift, agile flight in pursuit of prey. The pygmy falcons (genus *Polihierax*) display all the attributes for which their larger cousins are renowned. Weighing just 3¹/₂ ounces (100 g), the African pygmy falcon *Polihierax semitorquatus* is nevertheless a formidable predator.

CLASSIFICATION

ORDER FALCONIFORMES
3 FAMILIES
76 GENERA
300 SPECIES
FAMILY FALCONIDAE

Seen from below, the African pygmy falcon is mainly white.

Characteristics The sexes of the African pygmy falcon are distinguishable even when in immature plumage. The birds are light gray above and white below, including the forehead and face, but in females the back is a deep chestnut color. The flight feathers and tail are black, traversed by lines of white spots. The eyes are dark brown and the cere—the area around the nostril—and legs are orange. Immature birds have the plumage washed with light brown.

Feeding This falcon is a bold little predator, taking mainly lizards and insects, although rodents and birds are also eaten.

Reproduction Courtship includes the male feeding his mate. The falcon pair adopts a chamber in a nest of a weaver bird for breeding—the sociable weaver (genus *Philetairus*) in southwest Africa and the buffalo weaver (*Dinemellia*) in northeast Africa. The female does most of the

40 days' incubation of two to four white eggs, and also broods and feeds the young chicks. The nestling period lasts approximately 29 days, and the male provides most of the food to the nest throughout breeding. Pairs and families usually roost together in a chamber, in part to counter the cold desert nights.

Habitat This is a bird of semi-arid savanna with scattered trees in southwest and northeast Africa.

TINY RAPTOR
At only 8 inches (20 cm) in length, the pygmy falcon is aptly named. The bird shown here is a female, distinguished by the chestnut plumage on its back. Males are gray.

WHITE-EYED KESTREL

Kestrels, members of the family Falconidae, occur on all continents except Antarctica. Their usual hunting style is to hover above the ground in search of small mammals, which they pounce on with their feet. The white-eyed kestrel *Falco rupicoloides,* from Africa, is a typical representative.

CLASSIFICATION

ORDER FALCONIFORMES
3 FAMILIES
76 GENERA
300 SPECIES
FAMILY FALCONIDAE

Characteristics This kestrel is about 13 inches (33 cm) long. It is red-brown, with dark brown on the back, wing coverts and thighs, and streaked with brown on the head and upper breast. The flight feathers, tail and rump are sooty-brown with broad bars of pale gray across the feathers. The eyes of adults are cream; immature birds have brown eyes.

Feeding Lizards, birds, rodents, locusts and termites are the most important prey items, but any small animals may be taken, either from a perch or during bouts of hovering.

Reproduction Pairs perch prominently near their nest and proclaim their territory by high screams and fast rocking flights. The old stick-nest of another bird, often a crow, is adopted for breeding, and two to five eggs are laid. The female carries out most of the 32 days of incubation,

relieved briefly by the male when he brings her prey. The female also does most of the brooding and feeding of the chicks but, later in the nestling period, leaves them to help the male supply food to the young. Juveniles remain for about eight weeks in the parental territory before dispersing.

Habitat These birds inhabit grassland, steppe and semi-desert with scattered trees from Somalia south to South Africa.

SHARP-EYED HUNTER
The white-eyed kestrel can snatch small birds in mid-air. Like other kestrels, it also hovers on fast-beating wings as it scans the ground, looking for prey such as lizards and rodents.

STRIATED CARACARA

Caracaras are large birds with naked faces and large, powerful bills. The striated caracara *Phalcoboenus australis*, of the Falklands and nearby islands, spends much of its time on the ground, scavenging around seabird colonies or along the shoreline, or else looking for insects.

Characteristics This is a large raptor, about 24 inches (60 cm) long. It is mainly black, the somber color relieved only by white streaks on the neck and breast, and by a white band across the tail. The eyes are dark brown. The immature is sooty-brown with pale brown flight feathers and flecks on the neck. It takes approximately five years to assume full adult plumage.

Feeding The striated caracara scavenges around the summer breeding colonies of penguins and other seabirds, and for the rest of the year combs the beaches for

CLASSIFICATION

ORDER FALCONIFORMES
3 FAMILIES
76 GENERA
300 SPECIES
FAMILY FALCONIDAE

FAMILY RESEMBLANCE
The common caracara *Polyborus plancus* has the same large bill as the striated caracara. It ranges from South America to the southwest United States.

scraps or digs out insects with its strong legs. It also attacks weak sheep, introduced to the islands, for which it is persecuted.

Reproduction In summer, a small nest of grass is constructed on the ground among clumps of tussock grass or on rocky ledges. The eggs, richly marked in shades of brown, number two to four, and are laid on a lining of fine material including wool. Pairs may nest close to each other.

Habitat This caracara inhabits the seashore and adjacent interior of the Falkland Islands and small islands off the southern tip of South America.

An impressive bird in flight, the striated caracara nevertheless spends a great deal of time on the ground.

OWLS

These birds are more often heard than seen; their distinctive calls, described as startling, strange or weirdly beautiful, often carry across the countryside. They make up a well-defined group of nocturnal birds of prey, and even for people with little knowledge of birds, the members of the group are instantly recognizable.

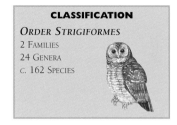

CLASSIFICATION

ORDER STRIGIFORMES
2 FAMILIES
24 GENERA
C. 162 SPECIES

LITTLE OWL
This little owl *Athene noctua* is nesting in the cracked roof of an old building. The species is found in Eurasia, north Africa and the Middle East.

Characteristics Owls are adapted to nocturnal conditions. Typical owls have large eyes with good vision in dim light, and barn owls hunt using their exceptional powers of hearing. Most species have soft, loose plumage, with fraying trailing feathers to the flight feathers of their wings and tail, for noiseless hunting flight. Owls have a sharp, hooked bill and strong legs and feet, with sharp, curved talons for their predatory lifestyle. Barn owls have a serrated edge on the talon of their middle toe, perhaps as an aid to grooming.

Feeding Owls feed by silently swooping down on their prey in poor light or darkness. They eat a diversity of small mammals, and also reptiles, birds and large insects; the fishing owls (genus *Scotopelia*) hunt fish. Owls

ORDER STRIGIFORMES
The owls are very widely distributed, from the Arctic to the far south, and occur in a great variety of habitats.

swallow their prey whole and regurgitate pellets containing the indigestible parts, including bones, fur and feathers.

Reproduction Owls nest mainly in tree hollows; the burrowing owl *Athene cunicularia* nests in burrows in the ground. In many owls, the young leave the nest well before they can fly; the parents continue to feed them for weeks, or even months, thereafter.

SHORT-EARED OWL
While most owls habitually hunt in poor light, they can see well by day and some, like the short-eared owl *Asia flammeus*, often hunt by day.

EAGLE OWL
The eagle owl *Bubo bubo* is the largest of all owls, measuring up to 28 inches (71 cm) in length and weighing as much as 8³/₄ pounds (4 kg).

BARN OWL

One of the most widespread birds in the world, the barn owl *Tyto alba* occurs in open cultivated country and lightly wooded areas in the Americas, Africa, Europe, Australia and much of Asia. Seen at night by the light of a car's headlights, the owl's white underparts, combined with its silent, hovering flight, give it an almost ghostlike appearance.

SILENT HUNTER
The barn owl hunts mostly on the wing, flying silently over the ground and locating its prey by sound only.

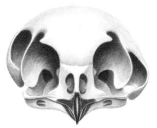

BUILT FOR STEREO
In some barn owls the ears are asymmetrical. Sounds reach one ear at a slightly different time to the other, enabling precise location of prey.

Characteristics The barn owl is 13 to 14 inches (33–35 cm) long. Plumage is mottled tan above, white below, and the bird has a pale, heart-shaped face.

Feeding At night, barn owls use their acute hearing to locate and capture their prey, mainly rodents.

Reproduction They nest in cavities in trees, barns and other buildings. The downy young molt directly into adultlike plumage.

CLASSIFICATION
ORDER STRIGIFORMES
2 FAMILIES
24 GENERA
c. 162 SPECIES
FAMILY TYTONIDAE

GREAT HORNED OWL

The low *hoo h-hoo, hoohoo* of this spectacular large owl is a familiar sound in much of the Americas, where the bird appears equally at home in woods and deserts. In some areas, the great horned owl *Bubo virginianus* is often seen perched at dusk on roadside phone poles, wires or even television aerials. In open country, these birds often use the perches that hawks use in the daytime.

The large ear tufts make the great horned owl difficult to mistake for another species.

Characteristics This owl's cryptic plumage varies in color from the pale, frosty gray birds of the Canadian tundra to the dark, heavily marked birds of the wet Pacific coastal forests. All great horned owls can be distinguished from other large owls by their widely spaced ear tufts, their fluffy white throat bib, and the dark cross-barring on their underparts.

Feeding Great horned owls eat mostly small mammals and birds, but fish, frogs, invertebrates and reptiles are also taken.

Reproduction These owls often take over the abandoned nests of other birds, especially those of hawks and crows. They also nest in cavities in trees or rocks. One to six eggs are laid.

CLASSIFICATION

ORDER STRIGIFORMES
2 FAMILIES
24 GENERA
C. 162 SPECIES
FAMILY STRIGIDAE

NIGHTJARS

The nightjars or nighthawks (family Caprimulgidae) are a large group and make up about half of the species in the order Caprimulgiformes. They have long, pointed wings and a swift flight, a wide gape, a stubby bill and a brightly colored mouth shown in threat. They are insect-eaters, active mainly at twilight.

A MID-AIR MEAL
Its gape at full stretch, this European nightjar *Caprimulgus europaeus* is about to make a meal of a large moth, caught in mid-flight.

CLASSIFICATION

ORDER CAPRIMULGIFORMES

5 FAMILIES
C. 24 GENERA
C. 102 SPECIES
FAMILY
CAPRIMULGIDAE

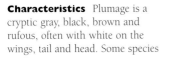

Characteristics Plumage is a cryptic gray, black, brown and rufous, often with white on the wings, tail and head. Some species

have long tail feathers, used in courtship. The bill is small but very wide. The legs are weak, much reduced and rarely used.

Feeding They feed on insects caught in flight in dim light.

Habitat Nightjars are widely distributed in the warmer parts of the world and have diverse habitat preferences. In Africa, for example, there is a different *Caprimulgus* species in almost every habitat.

ORDER CAPRIMULGIFORMES
The caprimulgiforms include the nightjars and frogmouths, as well as other, smaller families.

FROGMOUTHS

These members of the family Podargidae are the largest of the caprimulgiforms. They have been described as the most grotesque of birds, with a huge, flat shaggy head dominating the body, which tapers from it. But equiped thus, frogmouths are masters of disguise.

BLENDING IN
Frogmouths usually spend the day in a posture that enhances their resemblance to a tree branch.

Characteristics Like nightjars, frogmouths have cryptic plumage. The massive bill, surrounded by large tufts of facial bristles, as wide as it is long and heavily ossified (hardened like bone), acts as a heavy snap-trap. Frogmouths' legs are short and weak.

Feeding They pounce from a perch to catch non-flying animal prey in their massive gape and heavy bill; they batter the prey to soften it before swallowing it.

Habitat Frogmouths are arboreal inhabitants of forest, woodland and forest edge: *Batrachostomus* species occur from India to Malaysia; and the *Podargus* species in New Guinea, the Solomon Islands and Australia. The tawny frogmouth *P. strigoides* is found throughout Australia in most habitats.

FLIGHTLESS
AND
GROUND-DWELLING BIRDS

Although birds are the supreme exponents of flight in nature, many species have either lost the ability to fly or fly rarely. Why should this happen? The answer lies in the conservation of energy. Flight has a great energy cost. It requires large breast muscles and an elevated metabolic rate for those muscles to function properly. Therefore, when conditions permit it, if large breast muscles and an elevated metabolic rate can be eliminated, a bird will have greatly reduced energy needs. Less food would be needed, and more energy would be available for reproduction. The downside is that flightless and ground-dwelling birds are at great risk once humans interfere with their natural habitats.

OSTRICH

Ratites, the giants among birds, and their small relatives, the tinamous, are the living representatives of the order Struthioniformes. Members of this order—the ostrich, rheas, cassowaries, emu and kiwis—show that birds can evolve into large flightless vertebrates comparable with the large herbivorous mammals. The ostrich *Struthio camelus* is a giant among these giants.

TINAMOUS

Tinamous have plump bodies and short, rounded wings. The 45 species, found in Central and South America, vary from the size of a quail to that of a large domestic fowl. Many, perhaps all, species can fly, although they seldom do so; they usually escape predators by stealing away through cover or freezing. Tinamou species occupy a great range of habitats, including rain forest and the high and barren Andes. On the open tablelands, the martineta tinamou *Eudromia elegans* lives in flocks of up to 100.

BARE HEAD

An ostrich's head and neck are sparsely covered with bristly feathers. The eyes are prominent.

Characteristics Ostriches are the tallest of the world's birds. Males grow to 9 feet (2.75 m) tall, females to 6¼ feet (1.9 m). The feathers appear shaggy. Large concentrations of ostriches occur daily around water or where food is abundant, and immatures are found in flocks of up to 100 birds.

Feeding Ostriches eat a selection of fruits, seeds, succulent leaves and the growing parts of shrubs, herbs and grasses. They also take small vertebrates, such as lizards.

Reproduction Each cock builds a nest to which he attracts a hen. She lays her eggs there and

ORDER
STRUTHIONIFORMES
6 FAMILIES
15 GENERA
55 SPECIES
FAMILY STRUTHIONIDAE

becomes the "major" hen. Other hens ("minor" hens) also lay eggs there, but only the major hen and the cock incubate the eggs. She selectively keeps her own eggs in the nest, discarding some of those laid by the other hens. Eventually 60 or more eggs may be laid, but only about 20 are incubated. Both sexes guard the chicks which may remain as a family for 12 months.

Habitat The ostrich's range once included the Middle East, North Africa and Africa south of the tropical rain forests, but it is now essentially confined to various national parks in southern Africa.

ON THE RUN
Ostriches, like all ratites, are running birds. With their powerfully muscular legs, they can outpace most predators.

ORDER STRUTHIONIFORMES
All species are now restricted to the Southern Hemisphere, where they occupy a wide range of habitats.

EMUS

The Australian emu *Dromaius novaehollandiae* lives a nomadic existence, continually moving to keep in touch with its food—not that the food moves, but rather that abundances of insects and vegetation on which it feeds appear in random sequence in the Australian bush.

CLASSIFICATION

ORDER STRUTHIONIFORMES
6 FAMILIES
15 GENERA
55 SPECIES
FAMILY DROMAIIDAE

Characteristics Emus stand 6½ feet (2 m) tall and weigh up to 100 pounds (45 kg). Their brown plumage hangs like hair.

Feeding Emus move over vast distances, stopping when they find abundant food—flowers, fruits, seeds, insects, young shoots—and moving on when it is exhausted.

Reproduction After the female lays the eggs, the male incubates them alone. During that time he does not eat, drink or defecate, living instead on fat reserves. The male guards the chicks and leads them for their first seven months and sometimes longer. The female

BIRD OF MANY HABITATS
Emus are adaptable birds, living in a variety of habitats in Australia, from woodland to desert. There are thought to be about 500,000 of them.

SOLE SURVIVOR

The emu is the sole surviving member of its family. The King Island, Kangaroo Island and Tasmanian emus became extinct after European settlement.

RHEAS

South American ostriches The greater rhea *Rhea americana* stands about 5 feet (1.5 m) tall and weighs 44 to 55 pounds (20–25 kg). The lesser rhea *Pterocnemia pennata* is smaller. Both species have gray or gray-brown plumage, with large wings that cover the body like a cloak. When they run, rheas sometimes spread their wings, which then act as sails, but the birds are unable to fly.

Males at nest A male establishes a territory, then builds a nest, to which he attracts females, often as a small flock. Each female lays an egg in the nest, returning to do so every two or three days until the male, responding to the size of the clutch, drives them away and begins to incubate. The cock leads the chicks, which grow quickly.

may remain nearby, or move far away in search of food, or mate with another male.

Habitat Emus live throughout southern Australia. They become less common in the north of the continent, although a few birds can be found as far north as Darwin and Cape York. They are common in coastal scrub, in eucalypt woodland and on saltbush plains. A few venture into alpine heath, and many are still present in farming areas, provided some bushland remains.

CASSOWARIES

Cassowaries are jungle-dwellers. Three species live in New Guinea, and one of these, the double-wattled cassowary *Casuarius casuarius*, also lives in the tropical rain forests of far northeastern Queensland, Australia. They are not abundant anywhere, and their survival will be imperiled if the diversity of the forests in which they live is reduced by logging.

The colorful head and neck of the cassowary make a striking contrast with its plain, black plumage.

CLASSIFICATION

ORDER STRUTHIONIFORMES
6 FAMILIES
15 GENERA
55 SPECIES
FAMILY CASUARIIDAE

Characteristics The double-wattled cassowary stands 5 feet (1.5 m) tall and may weigh more than 120 pounds (55 kg). The other two species are smaller. Plumage is glossy black and hairlike, and all species have brilliant red and blue throat wattles. Two species also have a horny "casque" on the head.

Feeding Cassowaries depend on forest fruits for food.

Reproduction The clutch of six to eight eggs is incubated for about two months by the male. He also looks after the young chicks for about nine months before chasing them away.

Kiwis

There are three very similar species of kiwis: the brown kiwi *Apteryx australis*; the great spotted kiwi *A. haastii*; and the little spotted kiwi *A. owenii*. Restricted to New Zealand, the group has no close relatives anywhere in the world. All three species are flightless, nocturnal and live in burrows. And all three are listed as vulnerable.

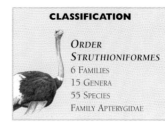
Characteristics Kiwis have a rounded body, with vestigial wings and shaggy plumage. The largest species, the brown kiwi, is 21 inches (55 cm) long .

Feeding Kiwis feed at night on invertebrates which they find mainly by scent, probing with their long and sensitive bills.

Reproduction The male excavates a burrow in which the female lays one to three white eggs. Each egg is equivalent to 25 percent of the female's body weight, proportionately the largest egg laid by any bird. The eggs are incubated by the male, and the chicks appear to be independent almost from the time they emerge from the burrow.

The brown kiwi is found on North, South and Stewart Islands.

PENGUINS ON PARADE

Penguins (order Sphenisciformes) are the most aquatic of all birds, some species spending three-quarters of their life in the sea. With wings that have evolved into paddle-like flippers, they are supreme swimmers. The 17 species display a diversity of adaptations to their aquatic life.

ORDER SPHENISCIFORMES
Most penguin species occur in the subantarctic, although some species range as far north as the equator.

SMALLEST OF ALL
The little blue or fairy penguin *Eudyptula minor* (below left) of New Zealand and Australia is the smallest penguin; 30 would be needed to equal the weight of an emperor penguin.

CRESTS AND BURROWS
The fiordland penguin *Eudyptes pachyrhynchus* (below left) of New Zealand belongs to a genus in which adults have prominent orange or yellow crests. The magellanic penguin *Spheniscus magellanicus* (below) nests in burrows along the coast of South America, from Chile to Brazil.

LARGEST OF ALL

Pairs of New Zealand's rare yellow-eyed penguin *Megadyptes antipodes* (left) nest in isolation, unlike most penguins. The chinstrap penguin *Pygoscelis antarctica* (center) inhabits the tip of the Antarctic Peninsula and nearby islands. The emperor penguin *Aptenodytes forsteri* (right) is the largest penguin—45 inches (115 cm) tall and weighing up to 100 pounds (46 kg).

Expert divers Penguins are by far the most accomplished of avian divers, and even smaller species such as the gentoo penguin *Pygoscelis papua* dive to depths of more than 500 feet (150 m). Penguins feed on fish, krill and other small invertebrates, and squid, which are captured and consumed under water.

Deep-freeze No other group of birds has to endure air temperatures ranging from -75°F (-60°C) during the dark Antarctic winter to more than 105°F (40°C) at the equator. Penguins depend on the insulative quality of their overlapping feathers to maintain body temperature, the dense waterproof layer effectively trapping warm air.

KING PENGUIN

Second-largest of penguins, the king penguin *Aptenodytes patagonicus* breeds on subantarctic islands in large, dense colonies, some of which exceed 100,000 pairs. It was severely persecuted by humans in the nineteenth century but is now increasing rapidly in number.

Now legally protected, king penguins were formerly exploited for their oil.

CLASSIFICATION

**ORDER
SPHENISCIFORMES**
1 FAMILY
6 GENERA
17 SPECIES
FAMILY SPHENISCIDAE

Characteristics The king penguin is some 38 inches (95 cm) long and weighs about 44 pounds (20 kg). It is a colorful bird, with a yellow-and-gold chest and black-and-gold head.

Feeding These penguins hunt in deep water for squid and fish.

Reproduction The female lays a single egg, which is incubated on top of the feet and covered by a muscular fold of abdominal skin. The chicks spend the winter in large groups known as creches where they are fed sporadically, and many perish.

ROCKHOPPER PENGUIN

The rockhopper penguin *Eudyptes chrysocome* gets its common name from the way it negotiates rock faces to reach its nesting sites on cliffs. Instead of waddling like a typical penguin, it bounds along with feet together, like someone in a sack race.

The rockhopper's yellow crest features in courtship and aggressive displays.

CLASSIFICATION

ORDER
SPHENISCIFORMES
1 FAMILY
6 GENERA
17 SPECIES
FAMILY SPHENISCIDAE

Characteristics This medium-sized penguin, like all other members of the genus *Eudyptes*, is characterized by prominent crests just above the eyes. In the rockhopper's case, the crest hangs out over the ears. The face is black and the bill orange-red.

Feeding These birds eat mainly small crustaceans caught at sea.

Reproduction The female lays dissimilar-sized two-egg clutches, and although two chicks may hatch, the adults are not capable of fledging both young.

Habitat They live in subantarctic waters and breed on island cliffs.

QUAILS AND PARTRIDGES

The more than 100 species of quails (Old World and New World) and partridges are part of the order Galliformes. Despite wide variation in size, all galliforms are characteristically stocky and have relatively small heads, plump bodies, short tails and short, broad wings. They spend much of their time feeding on the ground. Flight is fast and low.

Characteristics Old World quails are small, rounded birds with short legs and relatively pointed wings. The partridges are a much more diverse group: The very large, mountain-dwelling snowcocks which live in alpine zones from the Caucasus to Mongolia; the almost-unknown monal-partridges of China; seven species of red-legged partridges of Europe and the Middle East, adapted for life in arid regions; the larger francolins, predominantly of Africa; the spurfowl of Asia; the poorly known group of South-East Asian species that inhabit tropical rain forests; and the so-called "typical" partridges, which were originally natural-grassland dwellers of Eurasia.

Feeding A wide range of vegetable matter—seeds, fruit, buds, leaves—is supplemented by worms, insects and other small animals.

Reproduction Almost all quails and partridges are monogamous, and pairs with their immediate offspring form the basic social unit, a covey. The gray partridge *Perdix perdix* of Europe and parts of the Soviet Union has the largest clutch of any bird: 20 eggs.

Habitat Old World quails and partridges occur naturally from Africa east to New Zealand and north throughout most of Eurasia. Most species, however, are found in tropical Asia and in Africa south of the Sahara.

CLASSIFICATION

ORDER
GALLIFORMES
7 FAMILIES
76 GENERA
264 SPECIES
FAMILY PHASIANIDAE

CALIFORNIA QUAIL

The California quail *Lophortyx californica* of western North America belongs to the New World quails. Both sexes wear the unusually shaped topknot, but the female is otherwise much duller and browner than the male.

NEW WORLD QUAILS

These are typically plump, rounded little quails, often boldly marked and with distinctive crests. In the non-breeding season they are gregarious, forming coveys. The subfamily includes three species of tree quail of forests in Mexico and Central America; the barred quail (*Dendrortyx* species) of Mexican arid scrub and woodland; the mountain quail *Oreortyx picta* of woodlands of the western United States.; four grassland-dwelling North American species of crested quail; four colins or bobwhites; and 14 species of wood quail (*Odontophorus* species), forest-adapted birds of Central and South America.

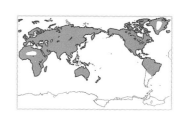

ORDER GALLIFORMES

This almost cosmopolitan order includes quails and partridges, grouse, turkeys, pheasants, peafowl and megapodes.

GROUSE

The more temperate zones of the Northern Hemisphere are the home of 17 species of grouse. In many northern areas, they are the largest year-round food source for predators, and their own numbers play an important part in determining the population size of some birds of prey.

RUFFED GROUSE
The ruffed grouse *Bonasa umbellus* inhabits deciduous woodlands and forests of North America, where it is fairly common.

CLASSIFICATION

ORDER
GALLIFORMES
7 FAMILIES
76 GENERA
264 SPECIES
FAMILY PHASIANIDAE

Reproduction
Reproductive behavior ranges from the strong pair bond of willow ptarmigans *Lagopus lagopus* to the displays of the male sage grouse *Centrocercus urophasianus*, designed to attract females for a few moments only.

Characteristics Grouse are plump, medium to large gamebirds with stubby, rounded wings and feathered legs.

Habitat Some live in coniferous forests, such as the spruce grouse *Dendragapus canadensis* of North America; others frequent more open habitats, such as the willow ptarmigan of Europe's moorlands.

TURKEYS

There are two species of turkeys: the common turkey *Meleagris galloparo*, native to the southern United States and Mexico; and the endangered ocellated turkey *Agriocharis ocellata*, confined to fragments of lowland rain forest in Mexico, Guatemala and Belize. It is believed that Mexican Indians were the first to domesticate the common turkey, which was later introduced to Europe.

Characteristics Turkeys are large birds, the males on average weighing about 17 pounds (8 kg), the females 8^1/$_2$ pounds (4 kg). They have strong legs, large spurs and almost completely bare heads.

CLASSIFICATION

ORDER
GALLIFORMES
7 FAMILIES
76 GENERA
264 SPECIES
FAMILY PHASIANIDAE

Reproduction Males gather at places known as leks where each performs a display, spreading his tail fans, lowering and rattling his flight feathers and swelling up his head wattles. In this posture the males strut around, uttering their *gobble gobble* call. Turkeys are polygynous (one male mating with several females), so dominant males achieve most of the successful matings at a lek.

Habitat These are forest birds, feeding on the ground by day and roosting at night in trees.

The common turkey spends most of its time on the ground, searching for nuts, seeds, berries and insects.

PHEASANTS

Most species of pheasants and their close relatives, peafowl and jungle fowl, are ground-dwelling forest birds. With the notable exception of the Congo peafowl *Afropayo congensis*, they all inhabit Asia.

Characteristics These are medium to large birds, often with long tails. All males are spectacularly colored and adorned with a rich variety of vivid plumes for use during their elaborate courtship displays. The crested argus *Rheinartia ocellata* has the longest tail feathers in the world. The males of the three peafowl species are famous for their train of decorated feathers, which they raise and fan during courtship.

Feeding These birds eat a mainly vegetarian diet of seeds, fruit, buds and roots, supplemented by worms, mollusks and insects.

CLASSIFICATION

ORDER
GALLIFORMES
7 FAMILIES
76 GENERA
264 SPECIES
FAMILY PHASIANIDAE

HUMANS AND THE JUNGLE FOWL

Close companions Gamebirds have a close association with people because their flesh is good to eat, but the closest association between any bird and humans occurs with the jungle fowl. The red jungle fowl *Gallus gallus*—which still lives in the wild in India and South-East Asia—was domesticated at least 5,000 years ago in the Indus valley, and since then has provided food (in the form of both eggs and meat) to almost every human race on Earth.

Most numerous The chicken is today found wherever people live, including on the high seas, and can be kept at much higher densities than other domestic animals. It may well be the most numerous bird in the world.

REEVES'S PHEASANT

Reeves's pheasant *Symaticus reevesii* is restricted to hill forests in central China. For many centuries its plumage (especially the tail feathers) was used by the Chinese as a decorative, ceremonial or religious motif.

Reproduction Each species has its own courtship routine, but perhaps the most impressive is that of the great argus pheasant *Argusianus argus*. The male clears a hilltop in the forest, from where he gives loud cries soon after first light to attract females. When a potential mate appears, he begins to dance around her, suddenly throwing up his wings into two enormous fans of golden decorated "eyes," which appear three-dimensional. The display culminates in an attempt to mate, after which the female will go off to nest and bring up a family, the male playing no further part. Most pheasants are either polygynous (one male mating with several females) or promiscuous. In some species, such as the ring-necked pheasant *Phasianus colchicus*, males defends a harem of hens, forming bonds with them until the eggs are laid. This social system, which also occurs in the jungle fowl, is rare in birds, although it often occurs in mammals.

PEAFOWL

The beautiful display of the male blue peafowl *Pavo cristatus* (also known simply as the peacock) is a familiar sight in many countries throughout the world where it has been introduced from its native India.

Characteristics The most striking feature of the peafowl is the male's elaborate fanlike train, which is more than twice as long as the body. The male's neck and breast are a beautiful metallic blue. The female is largely brown. Males utter a distinctive loud cry, particularly at dusk.

Feeding They feed on seeds, berries, green crops, insects, reptiles and small mammals.

Reproduction The male erects his train into a shivering fan as part of the mating display. No pair bonds are formed; each male mates with a number of females.

The gorgeously colored train of the peacock has but one purpose—to attract females.

Guinea Fowl

The seven species of African guinea fowl are large ground-feeding birds with long legs. Groups of the most widespread species—the helmeted guinea fowl *Numida meleagris*—regularly walk 20 to 30 miles (30–50 km) each day while foraging.

Characteristics They have largely naked, pigmented heads, with wattles and usually a crest or casque on top. Variation in the size and shape of these adornments, and the extent of naked skin, are believed to help the birds to regulate their brain temperature in different climates. The sexes do not differ obviously in appearance. Birds congregate in flocks outside the breeding season.

VULTURINE GUINEA FOWL

The vulturine guinea fowl *Acryllium vulturinum* inhabits arid scrublands in East Africa.

Feeding Guinea fowl feed opportunistically on the ground but roost, whenever possible, in trees.

Habitat All species live in Africa, mainly in semi-arid habitats, sometimes in forests.

CLASSIFICATION

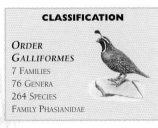

Order Galliformes
7 Families
76 Genera
264 Species
Family Phasianidae

MEGAPODES

Members of the megapode ("large-footed") family have unique nesting habits. They lay eggs not in conventional nests, but in burrows or mounds. Thereafter parental care is restricted to maintaining the mound in such a way as to ensure stable temperatures for the eggs. The eggs are incubated by the sun, by organic decomposition of plant material or even by volcanic activity.

Characteristics These are large ground birds with strong legs and short, broad wings.

Reproduction The male malleefowl *Leipoa ocellata* maintains a mound of sand throughout the year in which the female lays her eggs. It is the male's job to keep the nest at a constant temperature. Other species on volcanic islands lay their eggs in burrows where hot streams and gases provide the heat for incubation; one species uses hot volcanic ash.

INCUBATION DUTIES
The male malleefowl regulates the mound's temperature at a constant 91°F (33°C) by changing the depth of sand as necessary.

Habitat Of the 12 species distributed in Australasia and some Pacific islands, most inhabit rain forest and monsoonal scrub, but the malleefowl of southern Australia inhabits semi-arid eucalypt woodland.

CLASSIFICATION

ORDER
GALLIFORMES
7 FAMILIES
76 GENERA
264 SPECIES
FAMILY MEGAPODIIDAE

BUSTARDS

The bustards (family Otididae) belong to the same order as the cranes, the Gruiformes. They include 22 species of long-legged, short-toed, broad-winged birds of the deserts, grasslands and brushy plains of the Old World. The majority of the bustards are native to Africa; five species occur in Eurasia, and one is found in Australia.

CLASSIFICATION

ORDER
GRUIFORMES
12 FAMILIES
61 GENERA
220 SPECIES
FAMILY OTIDIDAE

FAMILY OTIDIDAE
Bustards are spread through much of the Old World, with the main concentration of species in Africa.

Characteristics
Mainly brown plumage gives cryptic coloration. Males are usually much larger than females and have ornamental plumes.

BLACK KORHAAN
The black korhaan *Afrotis afra* is confined to southernmost Africa.

Feeding Bustards eat vegetable matter, insects and small vertebrates.

Reproduction One male will mate with many females, and incubation and rearing duties are generally the sole responsibility of the hen. Three to five eggs are usually laid in a scrape on the ground.

183

OTHER
NON-PASSERINE BIRDS

The birds in this chapter fill just about every niche and habitat in the world, from the roadrunners of semi-arid regions to the turacos and parrots of the tropical rain forests. The enormous variation in the size of these birds—from insectlike hummingbirds to the great toucans of Amazonia—is matched by differences in plumage, bill shape, and social and reproductive behavior. Food requirements and feeding strategies vary, too, ranging from the woodpeckers, which drill into tree trunks to find ant larvae, to the swifts, which spend most of their time in the air feeding on insects. In short, the birds featured here demonstrate nothing less than the immense diversity of the avian world.

PIGEONS AND DOVES

Pigeons and doves of the family Columbidae are basically seed- and fruit-eating, tree-dwelling or terrestrial birds, occurring throughout the world except in the high Arctic and classified in more than 300 species. The term "pigeon" is used for larger species, and "dove" for the smaller, more delicately built ones.

NICOBAR PIGEON
The Nicobar pigeon *Caloenas nicobarica* feeds on the ground in the mangrove swamps and rain forest of Indonesia and New Guinea.

Characteristics The plumage is soft and dense, and the feathers have characteristically thick shafts and fluffy bases. The sexes are usually similar in appearance. Some species are brilliantly colored. Perhaps the most beautiful are the 47 species of fruit dove (genus *Ptilinopus*) of the Indo-Pacific region. These smallish, plump pigeons are colored with bright greens, brilliant reds and oranges, purples and pinks, blues and golds. Pigeons and doves have no, or very small, oil-glands—instead, special plumes disintegrate to produce a powder that cleanses and lubricates the plumage.

Feeding They feed on fruit and seeds, usually in trees, although some of the common species feed in huge flocks on the ground. Most birds take grit that lodges in the crop and helps grind up food, but

186

ORDER COLUMBIFORMES
This order, which includes the pigeons and doves and the sandgrouse, has an almost worldwide distribution.

SUPERB FRUIT DOVE
The aptly named superb fruit dove *Ptilinopus superbus* occurs in New Guinea and northeastern Australia. It feeds among the foliage of fruit trees.

fruit doves and imperial pigeons do not take grit, and have a thin gizzard with horny knobs which strips the flesh from the seeds.

Reproduction Pigeons and doves have characteristic sexual and advertising displays, such as bowing, and special display flights. All species build flimsy nests of a few sticks in trees, or on the ground or on ledges. One or two plain white eggs are laid, and the chicks are cared for by both sexes; they leave the nest in 7 to 28 days, depending on the species. The most specialized feature of the family is the ability to produce crop milk: When the birds are breeding, special glands in the crops of both male and female enlarge and secrete a thick, milky substance which is fed to the young.

Habitat About three-quarters of the 304 species of pigeons and doves live in tropical and subtropical regions. Some species are found only on single islands in the Pacific Ocean.

TURTLE DOVE

Europeans are familiar with this small, handsome dove. It is common in open deciduous woodland and groves in parks and countryside. The lazy "purring" of a turtle dove *Streptopelia turtur* is one of the typical sounds of a European summer.

CLASSIFICATION

ORDER
COLUMBIFORMES
2 FAMILIES
45 GENERA
320 SPECIES
FAMILY COLUMBIDAE

Characteristics This bird has reddish-brown upper parts, a blue-gray rump and distinctive white tail patches. Seen in flight, the dark underwings and white tail markings are distinctive.

Male turtle doves "purr" as a way of advertising their territory.

Reproduction Females build a nest of sticks in a tree or shrub.

Habitat Turtle doves range through Eurasia and North Africa, and winter in tropical Africa.

SANDGROUSE

Sandgrouse are medium-sized birds, specialized for a life in the deserts and semi-arid regions of Africa and Eurasia. They are very strong and fast fliers: The Namaqua sandgrouse *Pterocles namaqua,* of the deserts of southern Africa, can outpace a falcon in level flight.

CLASSIFICATION

ORDER
COLUMBIFORMES
2 FAMILIES
45 GENERA
320 SPECIES
FAMILY PTEROCLIDIDAE

PIN-TAILED SANDGROUSE
The pin-tailed sandgrouse *Pterocles alchata* inhabits North Africa, Spain, the Middle East and Central Asia west of the Caspian Sea. Flocks of at least 50,000 have been recorded at waterholes in Turkey.

Characteristics Sandgrouse have dull, well-camouflaged brown, gray or khaki plumage, and are compact and streamlined, with small heads and short necks. The tops of their feet are densely clothed in feathers. Males and females have different plumages.

Feeding They feed on seeds.

Reproduction They nest on the ground, and the young leave the nest a few hours after hatching.

DRIVEN TO EXTINCTION

Nothing symbolizes human mistreatment of wildlife and the need for conservation better than the notorious extinctions of the dodo *Raphus cucullatus* and the passenger pigeon *Ectopistes migratorius*. Coincidentally, both are members of the order Columbiformes.

The dodo's end The dodo of Mauritius was one of three species of massive, flightless birds on the Mascarene Islands, east of Madagascar in the Indian Ocean. Presumably, they derived from pigeonlike ancestors that flew to the islands. The dodo weighed about 50 pounds (23 kg). Its wings were reduced to useless stubs and it had no defense against, or means of escape from, the seafarers who killed it for food and sport. Discovered in 1507, it had been wiped out by 1680.

Dodo relatives The very similar white solitaire *Raphus solitarius* of neighboring Réunion Island was exterminated in the same way by about 1750, but the Rodriguez solitaire *Pezophaps solitaria* survived until perhaps 1800, and more is known about it. These birds supposedly laid one egg each year, were vegetarians, used their stubby wings for fighting, and were agile runners despite their size and gross proportions.

PASSENGER PIGEON
This bird once migrated across North America in hordes that darkened the skies. Nevertheless, the last one died in 1914.

DODO

This strange bird, about whose habits we know very little, was hunted to extinction by 1680. It probably fed on fallen fruit and leaves.

Passenger pigeon Like the dodo, the North American passenger pigeon was hunted to extinction. But unlike the dodo, this species was found over much of a continent and was incredibly abundant, possibly the most numerous bird in the world: When white settlers first came to North America there may have been three to five billion or more. One flock seen over Ontario in 1866 was 300 miles (480 km) long and a mile (1.6 km) wide and was visible for 14 hours.

The end The passenger pigeon was exterminated by relentless slaughter, just as the bison almost was. Birds were shot, trapped and poisoned in huge numbers. At one nesting site alone, 25,000 birds were killed daily in the breeding season of 1874. The last passenger pigeon died in Cincinnatti Zoo on September 1, 1914.

TURACOS

Turacos are gregarious, noisy birds, going about in parties of five to ten in forest and savanna, flying rather weakly from tree to tree, but running and bounding nimbly among the branches within a tree. They are rather long-necked birds with long tails, short, rounded wings, and erectile, laterally compressed crests, except in one species.

ORDER CUCULIFORMES
This order includes two families, the cuckoos (including roadrunners) and the turacos.

Characteristics The great blue turaco *Corythaeola cristata* is the largest species; all the other species are roughly the same size: about 17¾ inches (45 cm) in length and weighing 9 to 12½ ounces (250–350 g). Their feet are semi-zygodactylous (the fourth or outer toe is at right angles to the main axis of the foot and is capable of being directed backwards or forwards). Five species are dull-plumaged, grayish, brownish or whitish birds that inhabit savannas—the gray go-away bird *Corythaixoides concolor* is one example. The rest are brightly colored in greens, reds, purples and blues, which are formed by special pigments such as turacin, apparently unique in the animal kingdom. These brightly colored species typically live in forests. Turacos communicate with harsh loud, barking calls that can be heard from afar and may be recognized by other creatures such as antelopes as signals of alarm. In general, turacos are sedentary, or at least nonmigratory

Feeding Turacos eat mostly fruit, leaves, buds and flowers, but also take insects, especially during the breeding season.

Reproduction Their nests, always in trees, are simple, frail platforms of sticks. The young hatch at an advanced stage of development, and have thick down and open eyes (or nearly so). They are fed by regurgitation, and usually scramble out of the nest long before they are actually able to fly.

Habitat Turacos occur in forests and savanna in Africa south of the Sahara Desert.

CLASSIFICATION

ORDER CUCULIFORMES
2 FAMILIES • c. 40 GENERA
c. 150 SPECIES
FAMILY MUSOPHAGIDAE

WHITE-CHEEKED TURACO
The white-cheeked turaco *Tauraco leucotis* lives in Ethiopia and Somalia. It frequents dense brush and forest edges, feeding largely on fruit.

CUCKOOS

True cuckoos are members of the subfamily Cuculinae of the family Cuculidae, and are confined to the Old World. They are notorious for their habit of laying eggs in the nests of other birds, to be raised by the unwitting foster parents.

EUROPEAN CUCKOO
Cuckoos, such as this European cuckoo, are particularly fond of hairy caterpillars, which are despised by most other birds.

Characteristics Mostly they are drab, black and white, or black birds, with long, pointed wings. The smaller bronze-cuckoos of the tropics and Southern Hemisphere may, however, be brightly colored. Cuckoos generally seem to be solitary because the males are often very conspicuous and noisy with persistent bouts of loud, striking and rather monotonous calls, even at night, whereas the females are unobtrusive and have different, even muted, calls.

Feeding Hairy caterpillars make up a large part of the diet.

Reproduction The female cuckoo usually removes an egg of the host when laying her own; her eggs generally hatch earlier, and the young cuckoo evicts unhatched eggs or young of the host within three to four days of hatching. However, some large

CLASSIFICATION

ORDER CUCULIFORMES
2 FAMILIES • c. 40 GENERA
c. 150 SPECIES
FAMILY CUCULIDAE

ROADRUNNERS

Introducing roadrunners The members of the cuckoo subfamily Neomorphinae of the Americas, with one genus in Asia, are terrestrial birds, some of which rarely fly and some of which inhabit arid regions.

Greater roadrunner The best known member of this subfamily is the greater roadrunner *Geococcyx californianus* (right). It is about 20 to 24 inches (51–61 cm) long, with mainly brown plumage and a long tail. Typical of the southeastern deserts of the United States, it also occurs in open woodland, chaparral and farmland, where it runs

after snakes, lizards and rodents, which it kills with its stout, pointed bill. These birds can be seen early in the day perching on the tops of bushes, fence posts or rocks to sun-bathe—a way of warming up after a cold desert night.

species, such as the channel-billed cuckoo *Scythrops novaehollandiae* of Australasia, often lay several eggs in the host's nest; rather than evicting the host's eggs or young, the young cuckoos out-compete them for food, and they eventually

die. The eggs of cuckoos often mimic those of the host, especially if the host makes an open cup-shaped nest, and different females within one species of cuckoo may

each be adapted to parasitize one particular species of host.

Habitat Species are to be found in a variety of habitats, from open moorland in northwestern Europe to tropical rain forest.

Well-known species European cuckoos *Cuculus cuculus* are gray or gray-brown above and barred below. The female lays an egg in the unattended nest of a songbird. After disposing of other young birds in the nest, the young cuckoo grows until it is several times the size of its host parents. The high, penetrating, begging call of a cuckoo fledgling can sometimes lead the birder to the pitiful sight of a small bird feeding an enormous chick. Dependent on insects for food, European cuckoos have to spend the winter in tropical Africa.

SWIFTS

Swifts, with their compact, torpedo-shaped body and narrow, back-swept wings, are well adapted for a life on the wing. Not only do they have a well-deserved reputation for being among the fastest flying birds, they spend most of their time in the air, feeding, drinking and sometimes even mating in mid-flight.

BIRD'S NEST SOUP

Delicacy The main ingredient in bird's nest soup is the nest of cave-dwelling swifts, known as cave swiftlets, of South-East Asia. The nest mainly consists of the bird's saliva.

Renewable resource The nests are collected by men who climb bamboo scaffolding or vine ladders to reach the high ceilings of caves where tens of thousands of these swiftlets nest. Harvesting is controlled to protect the birds.

Characteristics

Swifts are mostly dark brown or sooty, with some areas of white or gray, and they have short legs with strong claws. A number of species, including the common swift *Apus apus* of Europe and the chimney swift *Chaetura pelagica* of eastern North America, make long migration flights to wintering grounds in the Southern Hemisphere.

TWO SWIFTS
The chimney swift (left) breeds in eastern North America. Its counterpart in the west is Vaux's swift (right) *Chaetura vauxi*.

The chimney swift originally nested in hollow trees, but has readily adapted to nesting in chimneys and other structures.

Feeding All species of swifts pursue and capture their food, mostly insects, on the wing. Sometimes the food ball or bolus taken to a nestling will contain up to 60 different kinds of insects and spiders, and several hundred

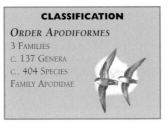
individual prey items can be found in a single bolus.

Reproduction Many swifts use secretions from their salivary glands in nest building. Some species nest in close association with humans and use buildings and bridges as nest sites.

Habitat Although most numerous in the tropical areas of the world, the 80 or so species of swifts are widely distributed, and even occur in Scandinavia, Siberia and Alaska.

SALIVA NESTS
The nest of the chimney swift is a half-saucer made up of small twigs glued together with saliva.

ORDER APODIFORMES
This order includes the swifts, crested swifts and hummingbirds. They occupy a diversity of habitats.

HUMMINGBIRDS

Hummingbirds are known for their small size, bright, iridescent colors and hovering flight. This diverse New World family, with 320 species in 112 genera, is most abundant in the warm tropical areas of Central and South America, but some are also found from Alaska to Tierra del Fuego and from lowland rain forest to high plateaus in the Andes.

Characteristics The average weight of these tiny birds is less than 1/3 ounce (3.5–9 g). The extremely rapid wing beat (22 to 78 beats per second), coupled with a rotation of the outer hand portion of the wing and a powered upstroke, permits hummingbirds to hover adroitly in front of flowers during foraging.

Feeding The shape of the bill reflects the type of flowers each species visits for nectar and

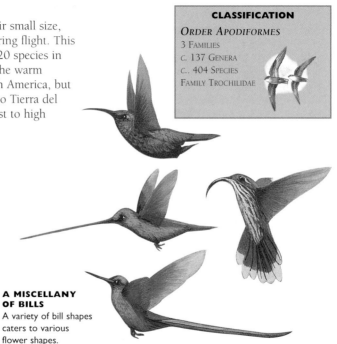

CLASSIFICATION

ORDER APODIFORMES
3 FAMILIES
C. 137 GENERA
C.. 404 SPECIES
FAMILY TROCHILIDAE

A MISCELLANY OF BILLS
A variety of bill shapes caters to various flower shapes.

HUMMINGBIRDS AT WORK
A hummingbird (unwittingly) carries pollen from one flower to the next in return for a reward of nectar. At left is the violet sabrewing *Campylopterus hemileucrus*; below, the beautiful hummingbird *Calothorax pulcher*.

insects. The sword-billed hummingbird *Ensifera ensifera*, for example, has a very long bill for probing tubular flowers. The tongues of hummingbirds are brush-tipped to aid in nectar acquisition, but insects provide a needed source of protein and are a major component of their diet.

Reproduction The breeding season of most species is keyed to the local flowering cycle. In most species the female alone builds the nest and incubates the eggs. Nests are typically small cups of plant material held together with spider web and sometimes adorned with moss or lichen. Some species build bulkier nests, sometimes attached to the underside of a leaf.

COSTA'S HUMMINGBIRD

Seeing a hummingbird in the field can be difficult, since they are small and fly at great speed. But patience can pay off, and then it is possible to see how tiny they are and admire their plumage and remarkable flight. One species worthy of a birder's time is this beautiful inhabitant of American deserts, Costa's hummingbird *Calypte costae*.

The male Costa's hummingbird has a characteristic purple throat patch.

Characteristics Costa's hummingbirds are between 3 and 3½ inches (7.5–9 cm) long. The male has an elongated purple gorget (throat patch) and fore-crown. Females look much like females of other small humming-bird species, and even experts have difficulty telling them apart.

Reproduction Males make high oval loops in a display flight, during which they make a high-pitched, thin, whining whistle.

Habitat Costa's hummingbirds inhabit the deserts of southern California and Arizona.

CLASSIFICATION

ORDER APODIFORMES
3 FAMILIES
C. 137 GENERA
C.. 404 SPECIES
FAMILY TROCHILIDAE

RUBY-THROATED HUMMINGBIRD

The ruby-throated hummingbird *Archilochus colubris* inhabits much of the eastern half of North America. Despite its tiny size, each year it embarks on a daunting trip south to winter in Mexico and Central America for the warm climate and ready supply of nectar-rich flowers, a migration that may cover more than 600 miles (1,000 km).

CLASSIFICATION

ORDER APODIFORMES
3 FAMILIES
c. 137 GENERA
c.. 404 SPECIES
FAMILY TROCHILIDAE

Characteristics These birds are approximately 3 inches (8 cm) long. The male has green flanks and a ruby-red gorget (throat patch). The female is green above and whitish below, with white corners to her tail, and lacks the male's red gorget.

Habitat This is the only hummingbird in eastern North America, and it occurs in woodlands, parks and gardens.

Reproduction During the breeding season, males display in front of females with a rocking, pendulum-like flight.

Like most hummingbirds in North America, the ruby-throated is strongly migratory.

TROGONS

These tropical birds of the order Trogoniformes are not well known, and there is still disagreement among taxonomists about details of their classification. What is not in dispute, however, is that some members of this order are among the most beautiful birds on the planet.

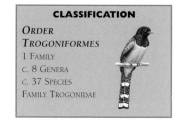

CLASSIFICATION

ORDER
TROGONIFORMES
1 FAMILY
c. 8 GENERA
c. 37 SPECIES
FAMILY TROGONIDAE

MOUSEBIRDS

Mousebirds (order Coliiformes), also known as colies, are superficially unremarkable in appearance, but they have some odd characteristics: They habitually perch in a distinctive fashion with the feet more or less level with the shoulders; their feathers are unusually fluffy; and they creep and crawl among bushes, clinging upside down, with the long tail held high in the air. They inhabit a wide range of country, from bushland to forest edge, in Africa south of the Sahara.

Characteristics Generally the head, breast and back are metallic, iridescent green with some reflections of blue and yellow. The belly may be carmine, red or pink, orange or yellow. Females are usually duller than the males, and Asian species are not as colorful. The tail is long and slightly graduated, usually with white or black bars. Quetzals (genus *Pharomachrus*) of Central America are well known for their long, drooping upper tail coverts.

Feeding Secretive and territorial, a trogon will perch, quietly scanning the area for food items, especially insects. With a slow, undulating flight it may snatch a caterpillar from a leaf or twig, then return to its perch. Occasionally small lizards are taken; and some South American species also eat fruit.

Reproduction Males may indulge in a display in which several gather to chase each other

VIOLACEOUS TROGON

The violaceous trogon *Trogon violaceus* inhabits rain forest edges and clearings from Mexico to Amazonia.

through the trees. The male calls to attract a mate to a suitable nest site. Females may answer; some remain silent. At each note the tail is depressed. Trogons nest in a cavity in a tree; some species excavate nest holes in dead trees. In the studied species, two or three rounded, somewhat glossy eggs are laid. The nestlings are naked and helpless when hatched, but soon acquire down. Both parents take part in the incubation and care of the nestlings and fledglings.

Habitat Trogons are pantropical birds of Africa, Asia, Central and South America and the West Indies. They are forest-dwellers.

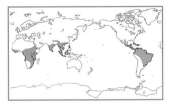

ORDER TROGONIFORMES

The trogons—sole members of their order—are found in forests along a wide belt of the world's tropics.

KINGFISHERS

Because the best known species of kingfishers (family Alcedinidae), the Eurasian kingfisher *Alcedo atthis*, feeds mainly on fish captured by diving into a pond or stream from an overhanging branch, the general belief is that all other kingfishers do likewise. In fact, most species are generalized predators that take a great range of prey from the ground or in water.

Characteristics A "typical" kingfisher bill is proportionately large, robust, generally long and straight, with a sharply pointed or slightly hooked tip. Kingfishers vary in size, from the laughing kookaburra *Dacelo novaeguineae* of Australia and the giant kingfisher *Ceryle maxima* of Africa, with a length of over 16 inches (40 cm), to the black-fronted pygmy kingfisher *Corythornis lecontei* of Africa at 4 inches (10 cm). Their plumage is commonly of bright

WHITE-THROATED KINGFISHER
The white-throated kingfisher *Halcyon smyrnensis* inhabits southern Asia from Iraq to the Philippines.

colors, often with a metallic brilliance, in blues, greens, purple, and reddish or brown tones which are frequently offset with white patches or dark markings. The wings tend to be short and rounded.

Feeding They feed on a wide variety of invertebrates and small vertebrates. The usual foraging technique involves surveillance from a perch, then a swoop or dive down to seize the prey, which is brought back and immobilized by being struck against a branch.

Reproduction These birds make their nests in natural hollows in trees or in burrows excavated by the birds in earth banks, termite mounds or rotten tree stumps.

Habitat Kingfishers are distributed worldwide, with the exception of the highest latitudes and remote islands. The center of abundance is South-East Asia and New Guinea.

ORDER CORACIIFORMES
The order includes kingfishers, todies, motmots, bee-eaters, rollers, hornbills, the hoopoe and wood-hoopoes.

CLASSIFICATION

ORDER
CORACIIFORMES
9 FAMILIES
47 GENERA
206 SPECIES
FAMILY ALCEDINIDAE

SPANGLED KOOKABURRA
The spangled kookaburra
Dacelo tyro of southern New Guinea is found in noisy groups, which frequent monsoon forest and small woodland patches. They generally keep to dense cover.

205

BEE-EATERS

As their name implies, bees—as well as other stinging insects—predominate in the diet of most species of these birds. Bee-eaters have developed an effective technique for devenoming their prey. A captured insect is struck repeatedly against the perch, and then is rubbed rapidly on the perch while the bird closes its bill tightly to expel the venom and sting.

Characteristics A slim body shape is accentuated by a narrow, pointed bill and a proportionately long tail, the central feathers of which are elongated in many species. Bright green upper parts are a feature of most species, and there are distinctive head or facial patterns. In all species the sexes are alike or differ very slightly, and young birds are generally less colorful than adults. Adults vary in size from 7 to 12½ inches (18–32 cm) long.

RAINBOW BEE-EATER
The rainbow bee-eater *Merops ornatus* is the only Australian representative of its family. It is strongly gregarious, and most populations are migratory.

Reproduction

The burrow nests excavated by bee-eaters in an earth bank or flat, sandy ground may be solitary, in groups of two or three, in loose aggregations spaced regularly or irregularly along a bank, or in large colonies. Incubation is shared by the sexes.

Habitat The 27 species occur only in the Old World, where the center of abundance is in northern and tropical Africa. Most live in open, lightly wooded country, often near waterways.

CLASSIFICATION

ORDER
CORACIIFORMES
9 FAMILIES
47 GENERA
206 SPECIES
FAMILY MEROPIDAE

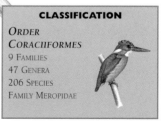

ROLLERS

Rollers take their name from the twisting or "rolling" actions that characterize the courtship and territorial flights undertaken by some of the dozen species in the family Coraciidae. These stocky birds have brightly colored plumage, with shades of blue predominating. They are especially prevalent in Africa, where both resident and overwintering species are conspicuous in open and lightly wooded habitats.

LILAC-BREASTED ROLLER
One of Africa's most conspicuous birds, the lilac-breasted roller *Coracias caudata* is usually encountered in pairs in open country.

CLASSIFICATION

ORDER
CORACIIFORMES
9 FAMILIES
47 GENERA
206 SPECIES
FAMILY CORACIIDAE

Characteristics Rollers are 10 to 14½ inches (25–37 cm) long, with robust bills and short legs. The squarish tail is fairly short, although some African species have tail streamers.

Feeding Some species catch large insects or small vertebrates on the ground, while others take insects on the wing.

Reproduction
Nests are in hollows in trees or in burrows excavated by the birds in earth banks, or sometimes in crevices under the eaves of houses.

HOOPOE

The first impression of a hoopoe *Upupa epops* in flight, bouncing and flapping with its rounded, black-and-white wings, is often of a giant butterfly. Once on the ground, however, this bird is often surprisingly difficult to relocate, as it probes with its long, downward-curving bill for insects and larvae in soft earth or cattle dung. The hoopoe is the sole member of the family Upupidae.

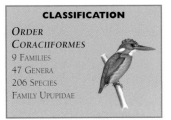

CLASSIFICATION

ORDER
CORACIIFORMES
9 FAMILIES
47 GENERA
206 SPECIES
FAMILY UPUPIDAE

Characteristics A large, erect crest and a long, decurved bill are unmistakable features of the hoopoe. The plumage is pink-buff to rich cinnamon or rufous, relieved by black and white banded wings and tail. The adult bird weighs about 2 ounces (55 g) and is about 11 inches (28 cm) in length. Hoopoes get their name from the territorial call of the male, a far-carrying *poo-poo-poo-poo*, usually produced out of sight in the canopy of a tree. During the breeding season it is usually encountered singly or in pairs, but at other times in family parties or loose flocks of up to 10 birds.

The crest is rarely erected, usually only when the bird is agitated.

Feeding It feeds mainly by probing with the long bill into soft earth, under debris, or into animal droppings for insects and their larvae—even in grazing pastures and well-watered gardens.

Reproduction Hoopoes nest in hollow limbs or holes in trees, in burrows in the ground, crevices in walls of buildings, or under the eaves of houses; they will also use nesting boxes. They

SIGNPOSTED ENTRANCE
A hoopoe female brings food to her chick. The entrance to a hoopoe nest is often clearly marked with droppings.

Habitat Widely distributed in Africa, Eurasia and South-East Asia, the hoopoe inhabits a variety of lightly timbered habitats where open ground and exposed leaf litter are available for foraging. The hoopoe is migratory in northern parts of its range, and partially migratory or resident elsewhere. Most migrants from Europe probably overwinter in sub-Saharan Africa. Populations from central and eastern Siberia migrate to wintering grounds in southern Asia. Though the species remains generally common throughout much of its range, there has been a steady decline in numbers in Europe during most of the twentieth century.

reuse some sites year after year. Only the female undertakes incubation, which lasts between 15 and 20 days. Newly hatched chicks are brooded and fed by the female, but later are cared for by both parents. The nesting hollow becomes fouled with excrement and remnants of food as the chicks grow, and the stench from one of these sites is not easily forgotten. Eventually the brood vacates the nest some 28 days after hatching.

HORNBILLS

Hornbills are one of the most easily recognized families of birds, the Bucerotidae. They are conspicuous for their long downward-curved bills, often with a prominent casque on top, their loud calls and, at close range, their long eyelashes. Most species have an unusual reproductive behavior involving the sealing of the entrance to the nest, with chicks and female inside.

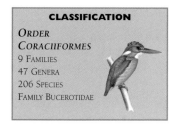

CLASSIFICATION

ORDER
CORACIIFORMES
9 FAMILIES
47 GENERA
206 SPECIES
FAMILY BUCEROTIDAE

Characteristics Hornbills range in weight from just over 5 ounces (150 g) to nearly 9 pounds (4 kg); males are slightly larger than females. The large bill serves a variety of functions, including feeding, fighting, preening and nest-sealing. The plumage consists of areas of black, white, gray or brown, with very few special developments apart from a loose crest, as in the bushy-crested hornbill *Anorrhinus galeritus*, or long tail feathers, as in the helmeted hornbill *Rhinoplax vigil*. However, the bill, bare facial skin and eyes are often brightly colored, with reds, yellows, blues and greens. The throat skin may form wattles, as in the yellow-casqued hornbill *Ceratogymna elata*, or an inflated sac, as in the wreathed or ground hornbills of the genus *Bucorvus*, or the whole head and neck may be exposed as in the helmeted hornbill. Each species also has a loud and distinctive call, from the clucking of von der Decken's hornbill *Tockus deckeni* or the booming of the Abyssinian ground hornbill *Bucorvus abyssinicus* in Africa, to the roars of the great Indian hornbill *Buccros bicornis* or the hooting and maniacal laughter of the helmeted hornbill in Malaysia.

Feeding Smaller species tend to be insect-eaters; forest-dwellers forage for fruit; and large, ground-dwelling hornbills feed on a variety of animals.

Reproduction All but two species are notable for sealing the entrance to their nest cavity into a narrow vertical slit, the incarcerated female and chicks being fed by the male. In most large forest species, the female remains in the nest until the chick is fledged, a total period of incarceration of four or five months.

Habitat The 45 species occupy habitats varying from arid steppe to dense tropical rain forest. Hornbills are confined to the Old World regions of sub-Saharan Africa and of Asia east to the Philippines and New Guinea. Toucans, some with relatively larger and more gaudy bills than hornbills, are their New World equivalents.

SOUTHERN YELLOW-BILLED HORNBILL

The southern yellow-billed hornbill *Tockus leucomelas* of Africa differs from most hornbills in its ground-foraging habits, and in feeding largely on insects rather than fruit.

PARROTS

Probably no group of birds is more widely known than the parrots. Indeed, one species—the budgerigar of inland Australia—rivals goldfish as the most popular pet animal in the world. Parrots belong to a very distinct order of ancient lineage, and are strongly differentiated from other groups of birds. There are two families: the Psittacidae (true parrots) and the Cacatuidae (cockatoos).

HAWK-HEADED PARROT

The hawk-headed parrot *Deroptyus accipitrinus* of Amazonia has a striking ruff of long, colorful, erectile feathers on the nape.

Characteristics Parrots are renowned for the generally brilliant coloration of their plumage. In most species, the sexes are alike, although females may be appreciably duller. Also characteristic is the short, blunt bill with a downcurved upper mandible fitting neatly over a broad, upcurved lower mandible. Parrots' feet have two toes pointing forward and two turned backward, allowing great dexterity when climbing or holding

CLASSIFICATION

**ORDER
PSITTACIFORMES**
2 FAMILIES
78 GENERA
330 SPECIES

DESIGNED FOR CRUSHING
The unique design of the strong, downcurved bill enables parrots to crush the seeds and nuts that constitute the diet of most species.

ORDER PSITTACIFORMES
Parrots are found predominantly in the Southern Hemisphere's tropical regions, especially rain forests.

food. The calls of most parrots are harsh and unmelodious. Prominent erectile head-crests distinguish the cockatoos.

Feeding Most parrots eat seeds and fruit foraged from treetops or on the ground. Lorikeets

(subfamily Loriinae) harvest pollen and nectar from blossoms.

Reproduction Parrots usually nest in tree hollows or holes dug in termite mounds, occasionally in holes in banks, or in crevices among rocks and cliff faces.

Habitat Parrots live mainly in the Southern Hemisphere, and are most prevalent in tropical regions. The strongest representation of species is in Australasia and South America. Parrots are particularly prominent in lowland tropical rain forest.

PARROTS' DAZZLING PLUMAGE

There are plain or dull-colored parrots, but these are few. For the most part, parrots are among the most beautiful of all birds, displaying a dazzling array of bright, glossy colors. This incredible spectrum is a vivid demonstration of the ways in which bird plumage gets its colors.

The black-capped lory Lorius lory *occurs in New Guinea.*

CAGED
The bright colors of scarlet macaws *Ara macao* make them popular cage birds. They are native to Central and South America.

What's in a color? Plumage colors are the result of the structural and pigmentary colors found in feathers. Structural colors are due to either interference with light (the result being iridescence) or the scattering of light, and the responsible structures are in feathers' barbs and barbules. Pigmentary colors are due to pigments. Many colors

A scarlet head and throat diistinguishes Australia's eastern rosella *Platycercus eximius*.

result from a combination of two or more pigmentary colors or from a combination of pigmentary and structural colors.

Camouflage Green predominates in most parrots, and is effective as camouflage in the rain forest canopy where many live. Bold markings, mainly of red, yellow and blue, are prevalent on the head or wings.

Blues, reds, yellows Unusual patterns are present in the *Anodorhynchus* and *Cyanopsitta* macaws and some *Vini* species, all of which are entirely or almost entirely blue, while bright yellow predominates in the plumage of the golden conure *Aratinga guarouba*, the regent parrot *Polytelis anthopeplus* and the yellow rosella *Platycercus flaveolus*. Some *Ara* macaws are almost entirely red.

Macaws (genus Ara) are perhaps the most gaudily colored parrots of them all.

215

WOODPECKERS

A typical woodpecker (family Picidae) clasps a tree trunk with strong-clawed feet, leans back to throw much of its weight onto its stiffened, spine-tipped tail feathers, and uses this tripod stance as a fulcrum from which to batter away at the bark with its rather heavy, chisel-like bill.

ORDER PICIFORMES
The order includes six families: barbets, woodpeckers, jacamars, toucans, honeyguides and puffbirds.

Characteristics Their stiffened tail, chisel-tipped bill, bony and muscle-cushioned skull, and long-clawed, strong toes enable woodpeckers to cling to the bark of trees and forage beneath it and also to excavate nesting and roosting cavities. Plumage is often some combination of black and white, and many species have patches of red on the head. The tiny piculets (genera *Picumnus, Nesoctites, Sasia*) of tropical America, Africa and Asia have

HAIRY WOODPECKER
The hairy woodpecker *Picoides villosus* is a widespread species of North and Central America. In winter, it sometimes visits bird feeders.

216

short, soft tails not used as a brace in "woodpecking," but these woodpeckers drum with the bill to communicate and do excavate their own nesting cavities.

Feeding Some species forage for wood-boring larvae, while others eat ants. The American acorn woodpecker *Melanerpes formicivorus* stores acorns in holes in special trees, to be eaten in the lean times of winter. The sapsuckers (genus *Sphyrapicus*) of North America make rows of small holes in the trunks of certain trees, where they regularly feed on the sap that accumulates and on insects attracted to it.

Reproduction Typically, a nesting cavity is dug into a tree trunk. Some of the flickers (genus *Colaptes*) nest in holes excavated in the ground or in termite nests. Soft-tailed wrynecks (genus *Jynx*) use natural cavities or old woodpecker or barbet holes.

Habitat Woodpeckers live anywhere there are trees in the Americas, Eurasia and Africa.

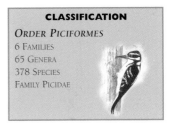

CLASSIFICATION

ORDER PICIFORMES
6 FAMILIES
65 GENERA
378 SPECIES
FAMILY PICIDAE

THE WOODPECKER'S TONGUE
The woodpecker's tongue is very long and can be extended well beyond the tip of the bill (left). It loops over and behind the skull to its anchor points in the hyoid bones of the jaw (right).

NORTHERN FLICKER

The northern flicker *Colaptes auratus* is the most common and conspicuous large woodpecker over much of North America. Its strident call, a loud *wick wick wick*, is a common sound in woodlands during spring. There are three subspecies: the yellow-shafted flicker of the east, the red-shafted flicker of the west, and the gilded flicker of the southwestern deserts.

Characteristics It has a barred, brownish back, and a bold black crescent across the chest. Males have "mustache" marks. Each of the three subspecies has variations in the color of the crown, nape and "mustache." The flicker is 10 to 12 inches (25.5–30.5 cm) long.

CLASSIFICATION

ORDER PICIFORMES
6 FAMILIES
65 GENERA
378 SPECIES
FAMILY PICIDAE

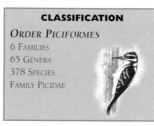

Feeding Flickers live in open woodlands and can often be seen feeding on lawns, searching with their long tongues for ants.

Reproduction The nest is generally a hole excavated in a tree, where three to ten white eggs are laid.

A black "mustache" identifies this bird as a yellow-shafted flicker, one of three subspecies.

GREEN WOODPECKER

In many parts of Europe and Asia, a loud, laughing call heard in the woods might be a green woodpecker *Picus viridis* disturbed at one of its favorite activities: digging in an ant hill for ants and their nutritious larvae.

ANT-EATER
The green woodpecker is always on the lookout for an ant's nest. It will break into one with pecking and twisting motions of its bill.

Characteristics The bird's upper parts are a deep green, and it has a yellow rump; bright yellow indicates a male, dull yellow a female. Both sexes have a red cap and a black mask. In size, the green woodpecker is about 12 to 13 inches (30–33 cm) long.

Feeding The green woodpecker spends much time on the ground, foraging for ants and ant larvae. Unfortunately, numbers of this species have decreased somewhat on the European continent, as acid rain has made its staple food more scarce.

Reproduction The nest is a typical woodpecker's, consisting of a hole dug into a tree.

CLASSIFICATION

ORDER PICIFORMES
6 FAMILIES
65 GENERA
378 SPECIES
FAMILY PICIDAE

RUFOUS-TAILED JACAMAR

The jacamars (family Galbulidae) are birds of New World tropical forests. They have longish, pointed bills and are insect-eaters, catching their prey in mid-flight. The rufous-tailed jacamar *Galbula ruficauda* is one of the most widespread and best studied members of its family.

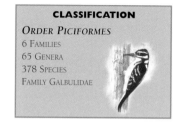

CLASSIFICATION

ORDER PICIFORMES
6 FAMILIES
65 GENERA
378 SPECIES
FAMILY GALBULIDAE

PUFFBIRDS

Puffbirds (family Bucconidae) are stout-billed, big-headed birds of South and Central America. Most are solitary species, but the nunbirds (genus *Monasa*) are social and even breed co-operatively. The black nunbird *M. atra* digs a tunnel nest into the ground, then covers the entrance with a pile of sticks, under which a horizontal tunnel leads to the nest chamber; adults in a cooperatively breeding group utter loud *churry-churrah* notes, answered by neighboring groups.

Characteristics The male rufous-tailed jacamar is about 10 inches (25 cm) in length. Prominent characteristics include a long, slender bill and a long tail. Its small feet have two toes pointing forward, two backward, an arrangement that aids grip and balance when perching in trees. It is metallic green in color with elongated central tail feathers, and generally rufous or chestnut below with a white throat. The female is similar to the male, but is buff-colored below and on the throat. They live a solitary life except when breeding.

Feeding This jacamar flies out from a perch and uses its slender bill to grab flying insects, such as wasps and butterflies.

Reproduction The male offers an insect to the female as a "gift" in courtship. The two of them excavate a nesting tunnel in a termite mound or earthen bank, and for about three weeks both parents incubate the eggs (two to four) during the day, the female incubating alone at night. The young hatch bearing whitish down feathers, and are fed insects. The nestlings make trilling calls, weak versions of the adults' notes. When leaving the nesting cavity about 24 days after hatching, the fledglings closely resemble their parents, sex for sex.

Habitat This species is less forest-dependent than most other members of this strictly American family, and it may be found even in grassland with scattered trees, as well as clearings, farmland and forest edges. This may account for its very extensive distribution from Mexico to northern Argentina.

GIANT HUMMINGBIRD
The long bill and tail, compact shape, and iridescent colors have led some people to call the rufous-tailed jacamar a "giant hummingbird."

TOUCANS

The huge-billed, comical-looking toucans of tropical America might be termed "glorified barbets," but of course their large size, frilled tongue, colorfully patterned and often serrated bill, and their inability to excavate a nest-cavity on their own, render them distinctive. They live in tropical forests and feed on fruit.

Characteristics Most toucans are black, blue, green, brown, yellow or red on the body, with brilliantly colored stripes or patches on the bill, and often bright, bare skin around the eyes. The function of the enormous bill is still uncertain, but it is known to be very light and the thin outer shell is supported internally by a spongy web of bony struts and tissue. In flight, toucans appear ungainly and conspicuous, but like parrots they are surprisingly inconspicuous when perched in a tree, unless they happen to be calling or displaying.

Feeding They adroitly feed on fruit, moving long distances from feeding tree to feeding tree, but can also pluck untended eggs or baby birds out of nests.

Reproduction Toucans nest in holes in trees, sometimes using the holes made by woodpeckers. Two to four eggs are laid.

HONEYGUIDES

Finding honey Predominantly African in distribution, honeyguides (family Indicoridae) are dull olive-green or grayish birds. Most species have a stubby or pointed bill, a very thick skin, and an ability to locate beehives. However, only one species, the greater honeyguide *Indicator indicator*, exhibits guiding behavior with a series of calls and flight displays that entice the local people to follow them to a honey source. The birds are able to locate and enter some hives on their own to feast on beeswax.

Hatchlings that kill Like cuckoos, greater honeyguides rely on other birds to raise their young. The female may destroy or remove an egg of the host when she lays; and when the honeyguide egg hatches, the hatchling has a pronounced bill hook with which it regularly strikes out, injuring and killing the host's young. When it leaves the host's nest the young bird seeks out wax in cavities of trees (abandoned beehives) and soon develops the ability to "guide."

SULFUR-BREASTED TOUCAN
Widespread in South American forests, the sulfur-breasted toucan *Ramphastos ambiguus* lives in small parties in the treetops.

Habitat Toucans are birds of tropical forests, and are found from southern Mexico, south through Cental America to northern Argentina.

Well-known species The collared aracari *Pteroglossus torquatus* lives in pairs and social groups from Mexico to northern South America. Its serrated yellow and black bill is a quarter of its length; the body is greenish above, with a black head, and yellowish below with two red bands, blackish in their center. These aracaris range through forests feeding largely on fruits,

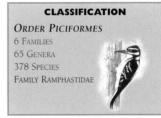

CLASSIFICATION

ORDER PICIFORMES
6 FAMILIES
65 GENERA
378 SPECIES
FAMILY RAMPHASTIDAE

calling *ku-sik* repetitively when moving about. They roost in old woodpecker holes, shifting from one to another at intervals, and also nest in such cavities. Sleeping in a group in one "dormitory," they are able to fold the tail over and onto the back.

223

BARBETS

Barbets are mainly birds of tropical forests, although some African species have adapted to drier conditions. These colorful birds are noted for their duets, sometimes conducted in groups which chorus together regularly.

Characteristics Barbets have generally heavy, pointed bills, some with a notch on either side. Plumage is generally colorful, and varies widely in color and pattern. A red cap, white facial stripes, olive back and orange throat mark the male scarlet-crowned barbet *Capito aurovirens*, which lives along the base of the Andes, from Colombia to Bolivia. Females are duller, with a whitish crown. African barbets are the most diverse, ranging from highly social (up to 50 or more pairs nesting in a single dead tree), dull-colored brown or olive species, to the group-social, duetting, multicolored species of the genus *Lybius*, and the solitary, tiny (length 3 inches, or 7–8 cm) tinkerbirds of the genus *Pogoniulus*. The gaudy red-and-yellow barbet *Trachyphonus erythrocephalus* is marked with black, yellow, white and red spots, stripes and blotches. Tropical Asian barbets tend to be larger than those in Africa or tropical America and are large-billed, large-headed, short-tailed birds. The numerous species generally are green with sexually differing intricate patterns of reds, blues yellows and blacks concentrated on the head and throat. Most belong to the genus *Megalaima*, and are solitary but highly vocal. The coppersmith barbet *M. haemacephala* is named for its ringing, oft-repeated notes—it is one of several diverse species called "brain-fever birds" because of their monotonous, unceasing song.

Feeding Barbets feed mainly on berries, fruit and buds. Some insects are also taken, and some larger species prey on small birds and mice.

Reproduction They usually excavate a nest hole in rotten trees, termite mounds or earth banks. The ground-barbets nest in holes excavated straight into the ground, or in termite mounds. Red-and-yellow barbets nest in groups, excavating holes in banks or termite mounds. Coppersmith barbets excavate a nesting cavity in a dead tree trunk or branch

Habitat Barbets are arboreal birds of tropical Asian, African and American forests and woodlands and (in Africa) arid scrublands.

RED-AND-YELLOW BARBET
Using its bright orange-red bill, the red-and-yellow barbet seizes insects, fruit and even young birds that it finds in the scrublands of Ethiopia south to Tanzania. It lives in groups.

PASSERINE BIRDS

A useful starting point in getting to know birds is to think of them as either passerines or non-passerines. The passerines are birds that belong to the order Passeriformes, which includes 5,000 or more species—more than half of the known species of living birds. Despite the great range of shapes and sizes displayed by passerines, these birds show much less diversity than the rest of the avian orders combined. It is also within this order that birdsong has reached its greatest development, and it was the passerines that French composer Olivier Messiaen had in mind when he said: "Among the artistic hierarchy, birds are probably the greatest musicians to inhabit our planet."

BROADBILLS

The 15 species of broadbills (family Eurylaimidae) are very colorful, with striking plumage and some having brilliant red, green or yellow eyes. They are chunky birds with broad heads and short legs and, as their common name suggests, they have broad, flattened bills. Broadbills inhabit tropical forests.

PITTAS

These beautiful birds resemble thrushes—indeed. they are sometimes called jewel thrushes. The 31 species, all in the genus *Pitta*, are distributed from Africa to the Solomon Islands and from Japan through South-East Asia to New Guinea and Australia. They are medium-sized insect-eating terrestrial forest inhabitants. When disturbed, they prefer to walk or run rather than fly. At left is the banded pitta *Pitta guajana*.

Characteristics Broadbills range from about 5 to 11 inches (13–28 cm) in length. African species are small, dusky birds. In South-East Asia, the green broadbills (genus *Calyptomena*) are superbly colored. Most species appear to be gregarious and move about the forest in small flocks, which could be family groups. In Malaysia, the long-tailed broadbill *Psarisomus dalhousiae* has been seen in flocks of 20 in association with "bird waves" totaling more than 100 birds of seven or eight species. The dusky broadbill *Corydon sumatranus* also joins bird waves; they have been observed sitting quietly on twigs, looking for insects while the flock passes, then flying on to join it and repeating the procedure.

Feeding Although most of them are mainly insect-eaters, hawking aerial insects in the lower canopy like clumsy flycatchers or catching them on the ground, they will also take small lizards and frogs. The diet of the green broadbills is predominantly soft fruits and buds.

Reproduction Broadbills' nests are masterpieces of camouflage. The nest is usually attached to a vine suspended in

CLASSIFICATION

ORDER
PASSERIFORMES
FAMILY EURYLAIMIDAE
8 GENERA
15 SPECIES

GREEN BROADBILL
The green broadbill *Calyptomena viridis* is a dazzling inhabitant of South-East Asian rain forests. It catches insects in the middle layers of foliage.

FAMILY EURYLAIMIDAE
The 15 species of broadbills are inhabitants of Africa, India and South-East Asia.

the open, often above a stream, where it appears as debris caught there at high water. This appearance is further amplified by a trailing tail of fibers or debris hanging below it, as well as decorations of lichen and spider

webs. Access to the nest hollow is through a hole in the side, which may have a short roof or vestibule.

Habitat Four species inhabit Africa; the rest are found in India and South-East Asia.

229

TYRANT FLYCATCHERS

The family Tyrannidae includes not only the tyrant flycatchers but also birds commonly known as phoebes, elaenias, kingbirds, flatbills and wood-peewees. Each species exploits the environment in a slightly different way, and so intricate is this division of resources that some avian communities in South America are known to contain more than 60 species.

Characteristics Tyrant flycatchers are small to medium-sized birds. The sexes look alike, generally with drab and inconspicuous plumage that is a mixture of greens, browns, yellows and white. The males of a number of species are adorned with crests. Tyrant flycatchers lack complex songs, although it is often easier to identify one of these birds by its call than by its plumage.

GREAT KISKADEE
The great kiskadee
Pitangus sulphuratus
is one of the most
conspicuous tyrant
flycatchers of
tropical America.

Feeding Although some species are fruit-eaters, the great majority of flycatchers, as their name suggests, eat insects. Each of the nearly 400 species employs a different combination of prey size, habitat, vegetation type, foraging position and capture technique. Ornithologists believe that it is this ability to finely divide the available resources, coupled with the fact that the New World tropics

CLASSIFICATION

**ORDER
PASSERIFORMES**
FAMILY TYRANNIDAE
114 GENERA
c. 400 SPECIES

MANAKINS

Forest birds Manakins (family Pipridae) are small, brightly colored fruit-eaters of lowland forests of South and Central America. The females look remarkably similar between species, most with green or olive plumage. In contrast, the males are generally brightly colored.

Courtship In a bizarre courtship display, the male wire-tailed manakin *Pipra filicauda* (above) rapidly brushes the female's throat with the wire-like tips of his tail feathers.

provide birds with rich and diverse resources to exploit, that gave rise to this largest of passerine families.

Reproduction There is a great diversity in these birds' reproductive behavior. In most species a strong pair bond is formed for the duration of the breeding season, and both sexes help to raise the young.

FAMILY TYRANNIDAE
The tyrant flycatchers are found throughout North, Central and South America.

COCK-OF-THE-ROCK
Cotingas, such as this Guiana cock-of-the-rock *Rupicola rupicola* are closely related to tyrant flycatchers.

Habitat These birds occupy a wide range of habitats, from open country and scrubby deserts to coniferous and tropical forests. The greatest diversity of tyrant flycatchers is found in the rain forests of the New World tropics.

LYREBIRDS

For those birders lucky enough to witness one, lyrebird displays are unforgettable—on the forest floor, the male's tail is fanned and thrown forward over the head and vibrated while the bird dances and sings. The two species are superb mimics, and an estimated 80 percent of a male's song may be mimicry of other birds—occasionally it may even mimic barking dogs.

FAMILY MERNURIDAE
The lyrebird family is exclusively Australian. Both species are restricted to the east coast.

Characteristics There are two species, the superb lyrebird *Menura novaehollandiae* and the smaller Albert's lyrebird *M. alberti*. They are pheasant-sized, with brown to rufous plumage, long, powerful legs, short, rounded wings, and a long tail with modified feathers; the outer two feathers in the superb lyrebird are shaped like a Greek lyre, hence the name. They are fast, agile runners when danger appears. They rarely perch in trees except to roost, ascending by jumping from branch to branch, and descending in the morning by gliding. The adult male superb lyrebird establishes a territory of 6 to 9 acres (2.5–3.5 ha) when sexually mature; the female's nesting territory may be within or overlapping the male territories. Males defend their territories, especially during the winter breeding season, by chasing intruders, singing, or displaying on earth mounds (well-concealed platforms of vines and fallen branches for Albert's lyrebird), which they have constructed throughout their territories.

Feeding The diet of both species is mainly invertebrates, such as worms and insects, which they expose by digging, ripping apart rotten logs, or turning over stones with their powerful feet.

Reproduction

The male mates with a number of females attracted to his displays. The female builds a domed nest, usually less than 6½ (2 m) feet above ground, incubates the single egg for 47 days, and feeds the nestling until it leaves the nest when about 50 days old. The young bird stays with its mother for about eight months after fledging.

Habitat The suberb lyrebird occurs in a narrow belt of Australia running from northeastern New South Wales to southeastern Victoria. It was introduced into Tasmania in 1934. Its habitat is wet eucalypt forest and temperate rain forest. Albert's lyrebird is restricted to a small belt of subtropical forest stretching from northeastern New South Wales to southeastern Queensland.

ON DISPLAY
To attract a mate, a male superb lyrebird spreads its tail into a spectacular fan and starts to sing.

CLASSIFICATION

ORDER
PASSERIFORMES
FAMILY MENURIDAE
1 GENUS
2 SPECIES

233

LARKS

Not all larks have the vocal powers of the renowned skylark *Alauda arvensis* of Eurasia, although many others sing well during their aerial song-flights. Some sing from tree stumps or posts or even anthills, and others produce clapping or fluttering sounds through wing-action during their nuptial displays.

SKYLARK

For protection against marauding birds of prey, Eurasian skylarks forage in groups. In winter, they gather in flocks of sometimes hundreds of birds.

WAGTAILS AND PIPITS

Wagtails The 60 or so species in the family Motacillidae can be divided into two groups, wagtails and pipits. Slender and graceful in build, wagtails are named for their habit of waving their tails up and down. They are mostly insectivorous.

Pipits Pipits are among the most widespread of all songbirds, found almost everywhere except Antarctica. Their tails are less developed than those of the wagtails.

Characteristics Typical larks are generally streaked brown over the upper parts, wings and tail, and white or buff on the underside, the breast usually streaked with dark brown. Some have a small crest on the head, and some show white over the lateral tail.

In most, the bill is slender and slightly decurved, but in others it is robust. The legs and toes are long. All walk rather than hop. The finchlarks (genus *Eremopterix*) are more variegated in their color patterns than true larks, and have short, conical, finchlike bills.

FAMILY ALAUDIDAE
Although the family occurs throughout temperate regions of the world, it is more prevalent in the Old World.

Feeding Larks feed on insects and other invertebrates, as well as seeds and grain.

Reproduction They build simple cup-shaped nests on the ground; these are sometimes completely exposed and sometimes sheltered at the base of a tuft of grass or under a low bush. In desert a partial canopy may be added to shield the incubating female from the heat of the Sun.

WOODLARK
The Eurasian woodlark *Lullula arborea* can be found near woodlands, in heathland, or in open country with a scattering of trees.

Habitat The lark family (Alaudidae) is centered mainly on temperate regions of the Old World in generally open habitats. It comprises about 79 species, with the greatest concentration in Africa. The most numerous is the shore or horned lark *Eremophila alpestris*, which has the widest distribution and occupies a great variety of habitats from Arctic tundra to temperate grasslands and even desert. Other species are usually more particular about their choice of terrain. Finchlarks inhabit semi-desert terrain.

CLASSIFICATION

**ORDER
PASSERIFORMES**
FAMILY ALAUDIDAE
c. 15 GENERA
c. 79 SPECIES

235

SWALLOWS

Swallows and martins (Hirundinidae) are small, slender birds that catch insects in midair, more or less sucking them up as they fly in graceful swoops, flurries and glides, usually at no great height over open ground. In some parts of the world they may be seen perched in twittering flocks along telephone lines when not feeding.

CLASSIFICATION

ORDER
PASSERIFORMES
FAMILY HIRUNDINIDAE
c. 20 GENERA
c. 82 SPECIES

Characteristics The plumage of typical swallows (genus *Hirundo*) is glossy blue-black on the upper parts, dark on the wings and tail, which is spotted sub-terminally with white. The outer tail-quills in adults extend into narrow filaments. Others may have the tail squared and lack the streamers of the *Hirundo* species; the top of the head and lower back are tawny or red-brown and the underside is streaked. The house martin *Delichon urbica*, and its allies the Asiatic house martin *D. dasypus* and the Nepal house martin *D. nipalensis*, distributed across Europe and Asia, are glossy blue-black above and have short legs and toes covered with feathers as a protection against the low temperatures they encounter. Other martins are robust, glossy

TREE SWALLOW
Pairs of the tree swallow *Tachycineta bicolor* take readily to nesting boxes. This species breeds in northern North America.

American species of the genus *Progne*, and the sand martins (genus *Riparia*), which are small and dull-colored. Most swallows and martins are strong migrants, especially the species of *Hirundo*, *Delichon* and *Riparia*.

PURPLE MARTIN
The male purple martin *Progne subis* is a glossy blue-black above and below, while the female is brownish with a pale belly.

Well-known species House martins are familiar birds in many parts of Eurasia (where they breed) and tropical Africa (where they winter). They are highly social and build nests in small colonies on buildings. The nest is bowl-shaped and made of mud. Aerial insects are their main food, which they catch as high as 330 feet (100 m). On summer days, their cheerful call, a babbling twitter, can be heard.

Feeding They feed on insects taken in flight, and some may be found consorting when insects are temporarily locally abundant. They may also be seen when insect swarms are present near the ground before a storm.

Reproduction Most swallows build solid nests in the shape of half-bowls, saucers and even retorts, fashioned out of mud pellets and straw, the eggs resting in a cup of fine grasses, hair and curly feathers. Sand martins nest in colonies, tunneling into vertical sandy banks and creating a nest of grasses and feathers at the end of the tunnel.

FAMILY HIRUNDINIDAE
The swallows and martins are distributed throughout most of the world's temperate and tropical zones.

CUCKOOSHRIKES

Cuckooshrikes are so called because of their bustle of hard-shafted yet soft and loosely attached rump-feathers, which is similar to that of Old World cuckoos, and their shrike-like bills. They are found only in the Eastern Hemisphere.

CLASSIFICATION

ORDER
PASSERIFORMES
FAMILY CAMPEPHAGIDAE
9 GENERA
C. 72 SPECIES

FAMILY CAMPEPHAGIDAE
Cuckooshrikes range through Africa, Asia, Australia and the Pacific. Many species are restricted to small islands.

Characteristics Cuckooshrikes in the genus *Coracina* are moderately large, gray or blackish and white, and generally barred. Males and females are similar in appearance. Their bill is relatively heavy, broad-based and hook-tipped, and they have short legs. Some species of this genus have a remarkable variety of forms—no fewer than 33 subspecies of the cicadabird *C. tenuirostris* are recognized. In the genus *Campephaga*, comprising five species, the adults are markedly different: The males are a glossy blue-black, some with bright patches of yellow, orange or deep red on the wings; the females are dark olive-brown, barred and streaked in yellow, yet whitish below. Cuckooshrikes are of secretive disposition, hiding among screening foliage as they forage for insects and fruit, but some *Coracina* species are more conspicuous and during the nonbreeding season may be seen in small parties. Other genera include the trillers (genus *Lalage*), which have blackish-gray and white plumage, with some tinged a rust color; the woodshrikes (genera *Tephrodornis* and *Hemipus*), which are gray, black and white in color, or else pied. Males of many species of minivets (genus *Pericrocotus*) are bright red, orange and yellow, and all females are less colorful than the males.

Feeding These birds eat flies, beetles, spiders and fruit. Caterpillars are the favorite food of some

BARRED CUCKOOSHRIKE
The barred or yellow-eyed cuckooshrike *Coracina lineata* occurs in rain forests of eastern Australia and the New Guinea region.

species, hence the family name, which means caterpillar-eaters.

Reproduction Nests are usually built high up in trees and skilfully blended into the moss and lichens of tree limbs to make detection by predators difficult.

Habitat Cuckooshrikes are found in the tropics of Africa south of the Sahara and also from Afghanistan and the Himalayas, east across Asia to the Japanese islands, and south to South-East Asia, Australia and the Pacific islands.

BULBULS

Bulbuls are a mainly tropical Old World family, Pycnonotidae, comprising 15 genera with about 120 species, which are distributed in Africa and from the Middle East across to Japan and south to Indonesia. The red-whiskered bulbul *Pycnonotus jocosus* has been successfully introduced to parts of Australia, and also to Florida.

RED-VENTED BULBUL
The red-vented bulbul *Pycnonotus cafer* is a common inhabitant of parks and gardens in South-East Asia. Its calls are cheerful but undistinguished.

Characteristics Bulbuls are small to medium-sized, and somberly colored in olive and brown, often whitish or yellow on the underside, with some exhibiting distinctive yellow or red undertail coverts. Many are crested and have hairlike "filo-plumes" over the back of the head. The bill is relatively robust, often notched towards the tip, and the legs and toes are strong. Vocalization generally consists of ringing calls, often in answer to one another from different points of the forest; and when breeding, the birds make short warbling and sometimes trilling songs.

CLASSIFICATION

ORDER
PASSERIFORMES
FAMILY PYCNONOTIDAE
15 GENERA
c. 120 SPECIES

FAMILY PYCNONOTIDAE
The bulbuls' natural range includes Africa, Japan and southern Asia. One species has been intoduced elsewhere.

LEAFBIRDS
The leafbirds (genus *Chloropsis*) of the family Irenidae occur in the forests of southern Asia. They forage for fruits, invertebrates and flower nectar in the forest canopy, where they are often difficult to see because of their dominant green color. Leafbirds are lively and dextrous, hanging upside down and assuming various acrobatic postures as they search for elusive prey and food items. The golden-fronted leafbird *Chloropsis aurifrons* (right) is noted for its mimicry.

Feeding Most bulbuls are insect- and fruit-eaters. When certain favored trees are bearing fruit, some species congregate in numbers, but otherwise they tend to be solitary and keep much to screening vegetation, especially in the canopy of high forest and woodlands. However, some exploit the understory and are partly terrestrial—especially so in the moderately gregarious species of *Phyllastrephus* in the African tropics. Several make their presence known in gardens in urbanized areas.

Reproduction Bulbuls build loosely constructed nests of local plant materials, placing them where they will be concealed in trees, bushes and creepers.

Habitat The main concentration of species is in the equatorial rain forests of Africa and similar vegetation in South-East Asia, the Philippines and the Indonesian islands. The Asian genus *Hypsipetes* has an extensive range, several species reaching islands in the western Indian Ocean.

SHRIKES

This family of medium-sized birds comprises three distinct groups: the helmet shrikes and the white-headed shrikes (subfamily Prionopinae, nine species); the bush shrikes (Malaconotinae, about 44 species); and the "true," predatory shrikes (Laniinae, about 25 species). The greatest concentration of species is in Africa.

CLASSIFICATION

ORDER
PASSERIFORMES
FAMILY LANIIDAE
C. 11 GENERA
C. 78 SPECIES

VANGAS

Mostly Madagascan There are 14 species of vangas (family Vangidae). All are small, tree-dwelling, perching birds which glean insects and lower vertebrate prey from trees. Only one species is found outside Madagascar.

Bills Vangas have a variety of bill shapes. The helmet bird *Euryceros prevosti*, for example, has a heavy bill which extends far back into the fore-crown; the sickle-bill vanga *Falculea palliata* has a scimitar-shaped bill.

Characteristics The true shrikes are patterned in gray, chestnut, black and white, and many of the African species are pied. The sexes are well differentiated. All species have a robust hooked and notched bill, and almost all are territorial and of solitary disposition. Most bush shrikes are attractively colored on the underside, especially the *Malaconotus* and *Chlorophoneus* species, which are largely green on the back, wings and tail, but yellow, orange or even red below. Helmet shrikes of the genus *Prionops* are characterized by feathering on the crown which forms a brush-fronted "helmet." There are also white-headed forms (genus *Eurocephalus*).

Feeding From a vantage perch, true shrikes watch for terrestrial prey, which is seized on the ground, and many are renowned for their habit of impaling surplus food items on the thorns of bushes or barbed wire fencing. Bush shrikes glean insects from tree limbs and foliage, but some species, such as the bokmakierie *Telephorus zeylonus* of southern Africa, forage extensively on the ground. Most helmet shrikes roam through woodland in parties feeding in the trees, although the white-headed forms feed independently.

Habitat True shrikes are characteristic of open habitats, preferring steppe—even when quite desertic—and lightly treed savanna, and virtually all of the birds that breed in the far north (genus *Lanius*) migrate to southern latitudes to avoid the winter. Bush shrikes occur in high evergreen forest or savanna woodland in Africa. Helmet shrikes are exclusively African and inhabit mainly arid scrublands.

SCHACH
The schach or rufous-backed shrike *Lanius schach* occurs across southern Asia from Iran to New Guinea. It is one of the true shrikes.

FAMILY LANIIDAE
The shrikes are primarily an Old World family, with only two species found in North America.

WAXWINGS

Waxwings (family Bombycillidae) are slender, elegant, crested birds with soft, silky plumage and yellow tail-tips. They are so sleek and trim that they seem as if they are carved from wood. These Northern Hemisphere birds are gregarious, and feed largely on fruit.

BOHEMIAN WAXWING
The Bohemian waxwing is larger than the cedar waxwing, and has a wider distribution, breeding in the forests of both northern Eurasia and North America.

Characteristics The name "waxwing" refers to a red, waxlike droplet that forms at the tip of each secondary wing feather, a decoration with no known use. There are three similar species: the Bohemian waxwing *Bombycilla garrulus* in North America, northern Europe and Siberia; the cedar waxwing *B. cedrorum* in North America; and a small population of the Japanese waxwing *B. japonica*, limited to northeast Asia. Waxwings are fawn-colored birds with a short tail, and they range in length from 5½ to 8¼ inches (14–21 cm). Except when nesting, they are highly gregarious; when perched on a limb or telephone wire, they stand almost touching.

Feeding All three species of waxwings feed heavily on cedar berries, and after the pulp is digested by the birds, the seeds are excreted—a very important element in reforestation. In summer, insects are often eaten.

CEDAR WAXWING

As well as inhabiting forests, these birds are frequent visitors to parks and gardens in North America, where they feed at berry-bearing trees and shrubs.

Reproduction The nest is an open cup, usually placed high in a tree. The female is fed by the male while she is incubating. Upon hatching, the nestlings are fed almost exclusively on insects until they fledge at 14 to 16 days. When nesting is completed, waxwings gather into large flocks and move south erratically.

Habitat The cedar waxwing occurs in both coniferous and deciduous forests, while the other two species tend to be more confined to coniferous forests.

Well-known species Cedar waxwings nest in northern North America, and move south in

FAMILY BOMBYCILLIDAE

Birds of this family breed in northern regions of Europe, Asia and North America, and fly south in winter.

winter (some reaching as far as Panama). These crested birds are 6 to 7 inches (15–18 cm) long, and have a narrow, black mask. Males resemble females in plumage, and juvenile birds have streaked underparts. Eggs are pale blue with dark markings. Cedar waxwings may be attracted to a garden by planting cedars (*Cedrus*) and rowans (*Sorbus aucuparia*), as the berries of these plants are their favorite food.

CLASSIFICATION

ORDER
PASSERIFORMES
FAMILY BOMBYCILLIDAE
1 GENUS
3 SPECIES

245

MOCKINGBIRDS

Mockingbirds and their allies are thrushlike birds of the New World. The family Mimidae includes 32 species of mockingbirds, catbirds, mocking-thrush, tremblers and thrashers, about equally divided between North and South America. The family is noted for its beautiful singers and mimics.

FAMILY MIMIDAE
The family is found from southern Canada, through Central America and the West Indies, to South America.

Characteristics They are sturdy-legged terrestrial or low-vegetation birds, with strong downcurved bills, short wings and long tails. Almost all species are gray or brown in color, but many have lovely patterns to distinguish them. The northern mockingbird *Mimus polyglottus* may imitate as many as 20 local bird species. All species are strongly territorial, especially the mockingbirds, which will aggressively attack transgressors.

FLOREANA ISLAND MOCKINGBIRD
The Floreana mockingbird *Nesomimus trifasciatus* is endangered in its West Indies island home.

These two Hood mockingbirds Nesomimus macdonaldi *of Hood Island, in the Galapagos group, have found an unusual perch.*

Feeding Most species forage on the ground, taking terrestrial invertebrates, which they find by using their downcurved bill to dig in the soil or search under surface debris. They also eat small fruits.

Reproduction Most build bulky, open-cupped nests of twigs, lined with grasses and fibers, in low vegetation. Incubation, mainly by the female but with the male's help, is about two weeks, and the young are fledged at about two weeks. Several species breed a second time each year.

Habitat They live in forest edges, swampy woodland, open country and desert habitats. Some species, such as the northern mockingbird, have colonized urban areas.

247

THE WORLD OF THRUSHES

There are species of thrushes (family Turdidae) in virtually every part of the world. The family is made up of two subfamilies—Turdinae, with some 175 species, and Saxicolinae, with about 155 species—and some of the avian world's best singers belong to them.

Subfamily Turdinae Included here are the typical thrushes, such as the American robin *Turdus migratorius*, the common blackbird *T. merula* and the olive thrush *T. olivaceus* of southern Africa. They are about 9 inches (23 cm) long, and soberly colored in brown with some gray or black. Most live in wooded areas, but they are commonly seen feeding both in trees and on the ground. Most species feed on fruits and animal prey, especially insects

WHITE-RUMPED SHAMA
The song of the white-rumped shama *Copsychus malabaricus* rivals that of the nightingale in richness.

and worms; those living in cold areas may vary their diet seasonally, taking fruit in fall, worms and snails in winter, and insects during summer.

Subfamily Saxicolinae
These are mostly smaller birds, such as the chats, wheatears and robins of the Old World, and the bluebirds of the Americas. They average 6 inches (15 cm) in

length. Many are more brightly colored, some having quite vivid reds and oranges, and the bluebirds being predominantly blue. A number of the wheatears are strikingly patterned in blacks, grays and whites. Many species, such as the nightingale *Luscinia megarhynchos*, are fine songsters with a rich range of notes. The subfamily occurs in a wide range of habitats, from forest and thick scrub to desert.

FAMILY TURDIDAE
Thrushes are found everywhere except in the Arctic, the Antarctic and some oceanic islands.

WHITE'S THRUSH
White's thrush *Zoothera dauma* is a comparatively quiet and inconspicuous inhabitant of the forest floor, where it searches for worms and insects. It has a very wide distribution, from eastern Europe, through China and Japan, to South-East Asia and Australia.

EUROPEAN ROBIN

The robin *Erithacus rubecula* is a bird of European woodland, parks, hedgerows and gardens, although in northern Europe it also occurs in luxuriant coniferous forest. The rusty-orange breast gives the robin an unmistakable appearance; the breast is a badge used in territory defense, not courtship. A repeated *tic-tic-ic-ic*, like the winding of an old clock, reveals this bird's presence.

Characteristics The robin is not shy but keeps close to cover, especially during the breeding season. In winter, both sexes sing a territorial song, and puff out their breasts to warn others from their area. Juvenile robins are brown with yellowish-brown spotting above and below, giving a scaly appearance. They molt in late summer into adult plumage, but a buffish wingbar still apparent in fall marks their age. British robins are sedentary, but migrants from northern Europe arrive in September to October and leave in early spring.

CLASSIFICATION

ORDER
PASSERIFORMES
FAMILY TURDIDAE
48 GENERA
C. 303 SPECIES

ADULT VERSUS JUVENILE
A freshly fledged juvenile robin (below), still lacking the orange breast feathers, looks surprisingly different to an adult (left).

Feeding They feed on insects and their larvae, worms, fruits and seeds.

Reproduction The female builds the ground nest of leaves and grass, lining it with dry roots. Three to six mostly white eggs are laid.

NIGHTINGALE

The nightingale *Luscinia megarhynchos* is justly famous for its vocal abilities. The song of the male is a loud, beautiful warble, usually performed at night and early morning, but also during the day. A characteristic phrase is a crescendo of whistled notes *lu-lu-lu-lee-leee*. The French composer Olivier Messiaen, who used birdsong in his music, called the nightingale "a great tenor."

CLASSIFICATION

ORDER
PASSERIFORMES
FAMILY TURDIDAE
48 GENERA
c. 303 SPECIES

Characteristics The nightingale is 6¼ to 6½ inches (16–17 cm) in length, with plain brown plumage; the slightly cocked tail is a reddish brown. Despite the distinctiveness of its song, this is a difficult bird to locate and observe, as it prefers dense thickets and damp undergrowth in woodlands and parks. The nightingale is highly migratory, and leaves Europe as early as August, to return in April or May from its tropical winter quarters in Africa.

TWO NIGHTINGALES
In part of its range, the nightingale (left) can be found with the very similar thrush nightingale *L. luscinia* (right), which is also a noted singer.

Feeding It forages on the ground for insects and worms.

Reproduction The nest is a cup of dry leaves lined with grass and placed on or close to the ground.

BABBLERS

The babblers make up a large subfamily (the Timaliinae) of the family Timaliidae, which is widespread in warm regions of the Old World. These typical babblers are small to medium-sized birds and are highly social. Most species are found in wooded country, many living in thick scrub where they are difficult to locate except by their noisy calls.

RED-BILLED LEIOTHRIX
Its colorful plumage and loud, melodious song has made the red-billed leiothrix *Leiothrix lutea* a sought-after cage bird. It is native to India and China.

Characteristics Most babblers are predominantly brown in color, although a few are brightly colored with reds, blues and yellows. There is little difference in plumage between the sexes. Most have multipurpose, thrushlike or warbler-like bills. Few have been studied in detail, but the following notes seem typical of many: They live in small parties of up to a dozen birds; they are highly social, and the birds remain together almost all the time; in

CLASSIFICATION

**ORDER
PASSERIFORMES**
FAMILY TIMALIIDAE
SUBFAMILY TIMALIINAE
49 GENERA
c. 255 SPECIES

SUBFAMILY TIMALIINAE
This subfamily occurs throughout much of the Old World. The majority of species are found in South-East Asia.

some species they roost together, sitting tightly packed along a branch. The group jointly defends the territory.

Feeding Most species are insect-eaters, hunting for insects or other small invertebrates among the foliage of trees or on the ground. The larger species also take small vertebrates such as lizards. Many will also take berries, and some feed on nectar when it is available.

Reproduction They breed communally, the dominant pair building a nest of twigs in a tree or dense bush; the remainder of the group help to defend the pair's nest and raise the young. Young males stay within their own group and breed either by inheriting the territory when their father dies or, if the group becomes large enough, by "budding-off" with some of the other younger birds into a new territory taken from a neighboring, small group. The young females disperse to other groups nearby, presumably to avoid inbreeding.

Habitat Although most babblers inhabit woodland, a few are more specialized to particular habitats; for example, the Iraq babbler *Turdoides altirostris* lives mainly in reedbeds and other swampy areas, and the Arabian babbler *T. squamiceps* lives in scrub along the edges of desert wadies.

PARROTBILLS
Parrotbills occur in northern India and South-East Asia, except for the bearded tit or bearded reedling *Panurus biarmicus* (below), which inhabits reedbeds from Central Asia westward into Europe. Parrotbills are small, brownish birds, ranging in length from 4 to 11 inches (10–28 cm). The majority have stubby bills, but that of the spot-breasted parrotbill *Paradoxornis guttaticollis* is particularly deep and rather parrot-like. They generally live in thick scrub, many of them in bamboo thickets.

WRENS

Wrens (family Troglodytidae) are small, drab, brown birds that usually inhabit undergrowth or very low vegetation. They are active and have high-pitched, vigorous songs. Many species habitually carry the tail cocked above the back.

Characteristics Most wrens are small or smallish birds, the largest being the cactus wren *Campylorhynchus brunneicapillus*, about 8¹/₃ inches (22 cm) long. They have short, rounded wings and are not strong fliers. All are basically grayish or brownish in color, many heavily streaked with black, and some have white eye-stripes or white throats. Many wrens have powerful voices, and some, such as the flutist wren *Microcerculus ustulatus*, are highly musical. Some sing antiphonally—a couple of birds giving responses, alternately, to each other.

Feeding Wrens are insect-eaters, and some species also eat small seeds and spiders.

CACTUS WREN
The cactus wren often builds its nest amid the spines of the chola cactus. It occurs from southern Mexico to the southwestern United States.

Reproduction All species build domed nests. Although most of the tropical species are thought to be monogamous, several of the North American species are polygamous, the males building a succession of nests in the hope

A lively, chortling song or scolding chatter often calls attention to the usually inconspicuous winter wren.

of attracting a new mate to each. The cactus wren lives in small groups in which juveniles of previous broods help their parents to raise the young of the current brood.

Habitat The wrens are a New World family, except for the winter wren *Troglodytes troglodytes*, which is also found in Eurasia, where it is known simply as the wren. Most wren species occur in South and Central America. Just nine species breed in North America.

CLASSIFICATION

ORDER
PASSERIFORMES
FAMILY TROGLODYTIDAE
16 GENERA
C. 75 SPECIES

WINTER WREN
The nest of the winter wren, built by the male within his territory, is a globular structure of moss, twigs and grass.

FAMILY TROGLODYTIDAE
Apart from one Eurasian species, the wrens are confined to the New World. Most species occur in the tropics.

WARBLERS

Most of the birds in the family Sylviidae are classified as Old World warblers of the subfamily Sylviinae. The majority of species are small, generally drab birds of forests and woodlands. What many lack in appearance, however, they more than make up for in song, being fine, strong singers. Many indulge in song-flights, soaring up and "parachuting" down in a striking fashion.

GREAT REED WARBLER
Like other reed warblers, the great reed warbler *Acrocephalus scirpaceus* lives in thick reedbeds. It has a rich and varied song.

SUBFAMILY SYLVIINAE
The subfamily has a wide distribution. The majority of species occur in Africa, and many also winter there.

Characteristics Most warblers are less than 6 inches (15 cm) in length, including the quite long tails of some species. Exceptions are the grassbird *Sphenoeacus afer* of South Africa and the *Cinclorhamphus* songlarks of Australia, both about 9 inches (23 cm) long. The majority are dull in color, mostly green or brown, although some are quite heavily streaked with black. In these the sexes generally look alike. An exception is the genus *Sylvia*; the males of many species are brightly colored, with orange or reddish underparts or black and gray patterning; females are duller. The bill is small and finely pointed.

Feeding The main food of almost all species is insects, which is probably why so many of those that breed at high altitudes or in northern latitudes migrate to warmer areas for the winter. Many warblers also take small fruits and berries when available, and a few take nectar or tiny seeds.

Reproduction Most Old World warblers are monogamous, but in some the males are regularly polygamous. For example, the male Cetti's warbler *Cettia cetti* may have as many as five or more females breeding in his territory. The majority build simple cup-nests in thick vegetation. The normal clutch is two to six eggs. The young are raised by both parents (except in polygamous species) and take two weeks to reach the flying stage, although in some species the young may scatter from the nest before that.

CLASSIFICATION

ORDER PASSERIFORMES
FAMILY SYLVIIDAE
SUBFAMILY SYLVIINAE
63 GENERA
c. 349 SPECIES

GOLDEN-CROWNED KINGLET
The golden-crowned kinglet *Regulus satrapa* belongs to a small genus of tiny, plump warblers characterized by a patch of vivid red or yellow on the crown.

FLYCATCHERS

Old World flycatchers of the subfamily Muscicapinae are small woodland birds with a distinctive habit of perching upright on vantage points and sallying forth to catch flying insects, often with an audible snap of the bill. Many species are brightly colored and highly migratory.

RUFOUS-BELLIED NILTAVA
The rufous-bellied niltava *Niltava sundara* is common in dense forests from the western Himalayas to Burma and Malaysia.

Characteristics Flycatchers are small birds, about 4 inches (10 cm) long, although some have long tails which make their total length much greater than this. They vary markedly in color. Many are rather dull brown birds, but in others the males are more striking—black and white, such as the collared flycatcher *Ficedula collaris*, or blue as in the Hainan blue flycatcher *Cyornis hainana*, or other colors. Most have rather broad, flattened bills.

Feeding These birds feed mainly on insects. Many literally catch flies, sitting conspicuously on perches and darting out to snap up passing insects. Others forage more among the foliage and take mainly perched insects or caterpillars.

Reproduction The flycatchers breed in a variety of sites. Many make simple cup-shaped nests

SPOTTED FLYCATCHER
The spotted flycatcher
Muscicapa striata takes readily
to nest boxes. This species
breeds in northern Europe
and Asia, migrating as far
as South Africa to avoid
the cold winter months.

treeless areas, avoiding the center
of deserts, high latitudes and high
altitudes. They are primarily birds
of wooded areas, from dense
forest to very open woodland,
almost anywhere they can find
an available perch from which
to hawk for insects. The orange-
gorgetted flycatcher *Muscicapa
strophiata* nests at 13,000 feet
(4,000 m) in the Himalayas,
where the forest is at its altitudinal
limits, but all depend on shrubs
or woodland of some sort.

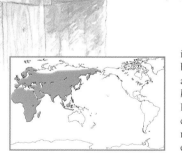

SUBFAMILY MUSCICAPINAE
These typical flycatchers are widely
distributed in the Old World, from
Europe to New Guinea.

in trees or on ledges on cliffs or
buildings, whereas others, such
as the pied flycatcher *Ficedula
hypoleuca*, nest in holes in trees.
Hole-nesting species lay larger
clutches than those of open-
nesting species—up to eight
eggs as opposed to two to five.

Habitat Members of the
subfamily Muscicapinae occur
almost everywhere except in

CLASSIFICATION

**ORDER
PASSERIFORMES**
FAMILY MUSCICAPIDAE
SUBFAMILY
MUSCICAPINAE
24 GENERA
153 SPECIES

FAIRY-WRENS

The main similarities between the fairy-wrens, grass-wrens, wren-warblers and emu-wrens of Australia and New Guinea (family Maluridae) and the wrens of the Northern Hemisphere are that they are all small and all cock their tails. Otherwise the two groups are quite different. The family includes 26 species in 6 genera.

Characteristics Male fairy-wrens (genus *Malurus*) are among the jewels of the Australian bush, tiny creatures arrayed in stunning combinations of turquoise, red, black and white. Their mates, and most other Australasian wrens, are more somber. Although the emu-wrens (genus *Stipiturus*), which derive their perverse name from sparse emulike tail feathers, do have blue bibs, and some of the secretive grass-wrens (genus *Amytornis*) have bold black and

SPLENDID FAIRY-WREN

The males of most fairy-wrens are clad in glittering blue, and this splendid fairy-wren *Malurus splendens* is perhaps the most striking of all. This species breeds in small groups in Australia's arid interior scrublands.

CLASSIFICATION

**ORDER
PASSERIFORMES**
FAMILY MALURIDAE
6 GENERA
26 SPECIES

chestnut colors, the overall design is for camouflage rather than display.

Feeding All are insectivores, and most forage on the ground or among the underbrush.

Reproduction Most members of the family are sedentary and build domed nests in dense vegetation. As with so many Australian birds, the young from one brood frequently remain with their parents to help raise later offspring. Detailed studies of species such as the superb fairy-wren *Malurus cyaneus*, a common bird even in suburban gardens in southeastern Australia, have shown that pairs with helpers are able to rear more young than those without.

Habitat The wren-warblers of New Guinea and some fairy-wrens occupy rain forest, where a few species venture into the canopy, but most members of the family are found in grassland or the understory of woodland. The Eyrean grass-wren *Amytornis goyderi* is confined to the sandhills of the driest of Australia's deserts.

FAMILY MALURIDAE
This family is confined to Australia, New Zealand, and New Guinea and its adjacent islands.

AUSTRALASIAN CHATS
Male Australasian chats (family Ephthianuridae) are boldly marked in red, orange, yellow, or black and white—colors that stand out in the swamps or arid open shrublands they inhabit—whereas females tend to be duller. These long-legged birds forage on the ground for insects. They are sociable, often occurring in loose flocks. The orange chat *Epthianura aurifrons* (right) undertakes extensive nomadic movements, in dry years sometimes irrupting from central Australia to areas nearer the coast.

MONARCH FLYCATCHERS

The family Monarchidae comprises more than 90 species in 17 genera. They are small songbirds with a predilection for flicking their tails and occasionally raising incipient crests, which give many of the species a characteristically steep forehead. The family reaches its greatest diversity in the tropical forests of New Guinea.

Characteristics Rufous, black, white, blue or gray, often with iridescent highlights, are the most common plumage colors of these birds, but spectacular exceptions include the black and yellow boatbills (genus *Machaerirhynchus*) and the paradise flycatchers (genus *Tersiphone*), in which the males have very striking, long tails which in some cases exceed 11¾ inches (30 cm) in length. Often the males have more brightly colored plumage than the females, but in many species the sexes are similar. The majority of tropical monarchs are probably resident within a territory, but those breeding in temperate regions—such as some populations of the Asiatic paradise flycatcher *Terpsiphone paradisi*, the black-faced monarch *Monarcha melanopsis* and the satin flycatcher *Myiagra cyanoleuca* of southeastern Australia—migrate to the tropics in the winter.

AUSTRALASIAN ROBINS

Like other members of the family Petroicidae, the red-capped robin *Petroica goodenovii* (right) looks a bit like the European robin *Erithacus rubecula*, but the two are unrelated. Australasian robins are mostly birds of woodland and forest where, rather than search actively, they like to sit and wait for prey to reveal itself. Breeding in temperate areas is in spring, and the nests are usually built with bark, moss and lichen placed in forks of trees.

CLASSIFICATION

ORDER
PASSERIFORMES
FAMILY MONARCHIDAE
17 GENERA
97 SPECIES

SPECTACLED MONARCH
The spectacled monarch
Monarcha trivirgatus is a bird of
rain forests and mangroves in
eastern Australia, New Guinea
and parts of Indonesia.

Feeding As their
common name
suggests, these
birds are insect-
eaters. In the
frilled monarch
Arses telescophthalmus there is a
difference in foraging behavior
between the sexes, with males
searching tree trunks
and females sallying after insects
in flight. Monarchs often forage
in mixed-species parties of birds,
which sometimes contain four
or five different monarch species
moving through the forest
together, the insects disturbed by
one bird being caught by another.

Reproduction
In temperate regions,
breeding is restricted
to spring, but it is extended
in the tropics. Their nests
are delicate cups sometimes
elaborately decorated with lichen.

Habitat Most are forest birds,
but there are representatives in
most wooded habitats in sub-
Saharan Africa, South-East Asia,
Australia and the Pacific islands.

FAMILY MONARCHIDAE
The monarchs are distributed from
sub-Saharan Africa, through India and
South-East Asia, to Australasia.

TITS

The true tits (family Paridae) are sometimes the most obvious small songbirds in parts of their far-flung range. Small, intensely active, acrobatic birds, many share a similar color pattern consisting of a dark cap, white cheeks and a small black bib across the lower throat. Some are familiar urban dwellers, and are among the most intensively studied bird species in the world.

BLUE TIT
Active, hardy, enterprising and entertaining, the blue tit is a popular visitor at garden bird-feeders across Europe.

Characteristics Few species exceed 5 inches (13 cm) in length. They tend to be brown, gray or green above, and paler or yellow underneath. The majority have black caps, some of them with crests, and white cheeks. The azure tit *Parus cyanus* and the blue tit *P. caeruleus* are predominantly blue above. They have short, straight bills; in many species these are slightly stubby and capable of hammering open small nuts. Those species that live in conifer forests have finer bills, probably associated with their habit of probing into clusters of needles.

Feeding They feed on a wide range of insects and seeds, although all bring insect food to their nestlings; many are seed-eaters in the colder times of the year.

Reproduction All species nest in holes, usually in trees, although some nest in the ground or among piles of rocks. Some use holes left by wood-peckers or natural causes; others excavate their own in rotten wood. Clutches range from three eggs in tropical species to large clutches in temperate species. The blue tit lays the largest clutch of any bird that raises its young in the nest—in central Europe an average of 11 eggs .

Habitat They are primarily forest birds. Almost all species occur throughout most of Europe, Asia, Africa and

In winter, the coal tit Parus ater (left) often joins relatives such as the great tit (right) in foraging parties in European woods.

FAMILY PARIDAE
Tits can be found in wooded regions of Africa, Europe, Asia, North America and part of Central America.

CLASSIFICATION

ORDER
PASSERIFORMES
FAMILY PARIDAE
3 GENERA
58 SPECIES

North America down into Mexico, but not in the rest of Central America. The majority of species are largely sedentary, although the most northerly populations of species, such as the great tit *P. major* in northern Europe and the black-capped chickadee *P. atricapillus* in Canada, may move considerable distances south to regions that have milder winters.

HONEYEATERS

The family Meliphagidae comprises about 167 species of honeyeaters, friarbirds, spinebills, miners and wattlebirds, all largely restricted to the Australasian region. New Zealand, New Caledonia and other Pacific islands each has a few species, but most family members inhabit New Guinea (about 63 species) and Australia (about 68 species).

FAMILY MELIPHAGIDAE
The honeyeaters inhabit Australasia, most species being found in Australia and New Guinea.

REGENT HONEYEATER
The regent honeyeater *Xanthomyza phrygia* inhabits dry eucalypt woodlands in southeastern Australia. It feeds mainly on nectar.

Characteristics One prominent characteristic is the unique structure of the tongue, which is deeply cleft and delicately fringed at the tip so that it forms four parallel brushes, an adaptation to nectar-feeding. Otherwise, honeyeaters vary greatly in size, structure and general appearance. All these birds are chiefly arboreal and normally gregarious, but there are very few features common to all. Honeyeaters are also notable in the range of social behavior that they exhibit. Some are gregarious only in the limited sense that they tend to gather wherever food is abundant, but many other species live in permanent, structured communities.

EASTERN SPINEBILL

The eastern spinebill *Acanthorhynchus tenuirostris* of Australia is abundant in thickets of flowering shrubs along the east coast and in Tasmania.

Feeding Some species inhabit rain forest, and these tend to feed mainly on fruits. Many others rely primarily on nectar, and yet others on insects.

Habitat This family forms one of the most prominent elements of the Australian songbird fauna, and it is there that the group reaches its greatest diversity, inhabiting virtually all habitats from highland rain forest to coastal heath and arid scrub in the interior. A birder

taking a casual stroll at any time in any Australian habitat can hardly fail to see individuals of several species of honeyeaters.

CLASSIFICATION

ORDER
PASSERIFORMES
FAMILY MELIPHAGIDAE
42 GENERA
167 SPECIES

FLOWERPECKERS

Nectar-feeders The flowerpeckers (family Dicaeidae) are widespread in southern Asia and Australasia. Most are dumpy little birds with long pointed wings, stubby tails and short conical bills. They feed on nectar, fruits and insects.

Pardalotes The pardalotes of Australia closely resemble flowerpeckers in size and proportions. They feed almost entirely on the larvae of leaf-eating insects, and the exudate made by these larvae, found on eucalyptus trees. Below is the tiny spotted pardalote *Pardalotus punctatus*.

267

TANAGERS

The tanagers (subfamily Thraupinae), about 240 species in 58 genera, are entirely New World in distribution. Although a few species are drab and secretive, the tanagers include some of the most colorful of all birds, especially in the genus *Tangara*.

Characteristics Tanagers are small to medium-sized birds with slender bills. Most species are brightly colored; the paradise tanager *Tangara chilensis* is particularly beautiful in bright shades of sky blue and navy blue, with a green mask and a yellow and red rump.

Feeding Most are primarily fruit-eaters but they also take insects. Some, such as the honeycreepers (genera *Cyanerpes* and *Dacnis*) and the flower-piercers (*Diglossa*), are nectar specialists and have long, thin, delicate bills. A few (for example, the genera *Lanio* and *Habia*) are insect specialists, and have heavy bills equipped with notches to better grasp insects. Some tanagers are noted for their behavior of following troops of army ants that stir up insects in their wake.

RED-LEGGED HONEYCREEPER
The red-legged honeycreeper *Cyanerpes cyaneus* is widespread from Mexico to central Brazil. This gregarious forest bird feeds on nectar, fruits and small insects.

CLASSIFICATION

ORDER
PASSERIFORMES
FAMILY EMBERIZIDAE
SUBFAMILY
THRAUPINAE
58 GENERA
c. 240 SPECIES

Reproduction Most tanagers build cup-shaped nests placed among moss or dead leaves. Others, such as the *Euphonia* and *Chlorophonia* species, build globular nests. The female does most of the nest-building and incubation. Some males may feed the incubating female, and both sexes feed the young. Incubation is shorter (10 to 13 days) for the open cup-nesters, which are subject to higher predation rates, and longer (18 to 24 days) for the *Euphonia* species, which build domed, camouflaged nests. Breeding pairs and their broods form small post-breeding flocks of up to a dozen individuals.

Habitat Four species (genus *Piranga*) breed in the United States and migrate to the tropics in the fall; some 163 species are confined to South America. Most (about 149 species) are forest-dwellers, whereas others (about 54 species) tend to prefer semi-open areas; the rest of the species do not show obvious habitat preferences.

SUBFAMILY THRAUPINAE
The tanagers are found only in the Americas. The Andes is the center of radiation for the group.

SUPERB TANAGER
The superb tanager *Tangara fastuosa* is confined to the forests of Brazil.

WOOD WARBLERS

Wood warblers (family Parulidae) reach their greatest diversity in North America, Central America and the West Indies; about 13 species and many additional subspecies are actually confined to islands in the West Indies. However, these small insect-eaters occupy virtually every conceivable habitat south of the tundra.

CHESTNUT-SIDED WARBLER
When it molts in late summer, this chestnut-sided warbler *Dendroica pensylvanica* will lose much of its color, becoming quite gray and drab.

Characteristics Most of the wood warblers are brightly colored and patterned. Among the North American species, males in the breeding season are often more brilliantly colored than females, but both sexes usually molt into a less conspicuous plumage before the autumn migration, similar to the plumage of their young; in fall, many conspicuous details of the breeding plumage are lost, so these species present notorious identification problems for birders.

Feeding Although primarily insect-eaters, wood warblers exhibit many foraging methods. Some are excellent flycatchers and have evolved the flatter bills, surrounded by longer hairlike rictal bristles, typical of birds that forage aerially. Narrow, thin bills exemplify the many species that pick small insects or their eggs from leaves or twigs.

One species, the black-and-white warbler *Mniotilta varia* of eastern North America, has creeperlike habits—climbing on trunks and limbs of trees to search crevices in the bark for small insects and

FAMILY PARULIDAE
Wood warblers occur from northern North America south through Central America to southern Argentina.

eggs—and has evolved a bill, toes and claws longer than those of its nearest relatives.

Reproduction Most nest in trees, shrubs or vines; those that nest on the ground tend to do so in wooded habitats rather than open country.

Habitat Several species of wood warblers are typical of the vast belt of coniferous forest

stretching across Canada and the northern United States, extending south in the mountains to Mexico. Others prefer deciduous and mixed forests. The yellowthroats of the genus *Geothlypis* are unusual in nesting in marshes and upland areas that may lack any woody vegetation.

COMMON YELLOWTHROAT
An immature common yellowthroat *Geothlypis trichas* (left) looks much like an adult female (right).

CLASSIFICATION

ORDER PASSERIFORMES
FAMILY PARULIDAE
22 GENERA
114 SPECIES

ORANGE-CROWNED WARBLER

Like many species with a widespread range in North America, the orange-crowned warbler *Vermivora celata* shows marked regional variation in its plumage: Western birds are brightest, and can be a strong yellow overall, while eastern birds tend to be a duller, grayish olive overall and have a gray hood.

The western form of the orange-crowned warbler (left) is noticeably brighter than the eastern form (right).

Characteristics This bird is about 5 inches (12.5 cm) long with a sharply pointed bill. It lacks bold wing and tail markings, and the orange crown patch is usually concealed. Its song is a rapid trill that fades abruptly. Two useful field marks are the face pattern (pale, narrow eyebrows and pale eye-crescents), and the bright yellow undertail coverts.

Reproduction The orange-crowned warbler's nest is a cup of fine grass, spider's silk and bark strips suspended in a fork in the middle to upper levels of a tree. Three to five eggs are laid; they are white with reddish brown flecks.

Habitat It favors brushy woodland, forest edges and chaparral.

CLASSIFICATION

ORDER
PASSERIFORMES
FAMILY PARULIDAE
22 GENERA
114 SPECIES

YELLOW WARBLER

One of the most widespread warblers in North America in summer, the yellow warbler *Dendroica petechia* nests in woodlands, groves of willows and alders, and orchards, often near water. Its bright song has been phrased by birders as *sweet sweet sweet, I'm so sweet*.

CLASSIFICATION

ORDER
PASSERIFORMES
FAMILY PARULIDAE
22 GENERA
114 SPECIES

Characteristics It is a well-named bird, the male's face and underparts being bright yellow. The reddish streaks on the male's chest are a good field mark. The female is duller than the male but is still yellowish overall, her head and upper parts washed with olive. It has a blank-looking face with a yellowish eye-ring.

Reproduction The nest is a cup of grass and lichens positioned at the middle to upper levels of a tree. Three to six eggs are laid.

Habitat This bird breeds in most of North America, and winters in Central America and northern South America.

The yellow warbler (right) is similar to the Wilson's warbler Wilsonia pusilla (center) and the orange-crowned warbler Vermivora celata (left). Telling these species apart is often difficult.

ICTERIDS

The most morphologically and ecologically diverse group of the New World songbirds is the family Icteridae, for which there is no really good comprehensive English name. Often called "American blackbirds," relatively few of its 92 or so species are wholly or predominantly black. The family includes the cowbirds, caciques, grackles, orioles, American blackbirds and meadowlarks.

GREAT-TAILED GRACKLE
Large, noisy roosts of the great-tailed grackle are typical of towns and villages in Mexico and Central America.

Characteristics This family has a greater range of sizes among species than any other family in the order Passeriformes. Size difference between the sexes is especially conspicuous, particularly in the larger species—the male great-tailed grackle *Quiscalus mexicanus* may weigh as much as 60 percent more than the female.

Feeding The diet of this family varies greatly. In general, though, all species feed on insects, and most eat seeds and grains.

Reproduction Nesting habits are diverse. Some of the caciques, oropendolas and marsh-inhabiting blackbirds nest in dense colonies.

Only one of the six species of cowbirds builds its own nest; all of the others are parasitic, depositing eggs in the nests of other birds.

FAMILY ICTERIDAE
The icterids are found wholly within the New World, mainly in the tropics, in virtually all habitats.

BOBOLINK
The bobolink *Dolichonyx oryzivorus* breeds in grainfields and marshlands in North America, and winters in South America. This is the female.

Habitat The family is mostly tropical, although it has many representatives in temperate regions. Except for some of the oropendolas and caciques, relatively few species are true forest birds. Many inhabit swamps, marshes and savannas, and many of the orioles prefer open woodlands and scrub. Some grackles have become urbanized; the common grackle *Quiscalus quiscula* is abundant in city parks in much of the United States and Canada.

CLASSIFICATION

ORDER
PASSERIFORMES
FAMILY ICTERIDAE
25 GENERA
92 SPECIES

NORTHERN ORIOLE
A female northern oriole *Icterus galbula* sees to her chicks. She belongs to the Baltimore race, which was once considered a separate species.

STARLINGS

Starlings (family Sturnidae) are Old World birds, with strongest representation in hotter climates. A number of species have glossy black plumage, but many are boldy patterned and brilliantly colored. The family includes one of the most widespread and widely recognized of all birds, the common starling *Sturnus vulgaris*.

CLASSIFICATION

ORDER
PASSERIFORMES
FAMILY STURNIDAE
27 GENERA
113 SPECIES

Characteristics These are mainly small to medium-sized birds with strong bills and legs. Most species are gregarious, and many roost in flocks. The common starling is fairly typical of the family. It is a stumpy, rather short-tailed bird with a confident strut and an alert, pugnacious manner. The 35 African species of starlings include some strikingly beautiful birds with glossy, iridescent plumage, often featuring patches of vivid violet, green, orange and

blue. The mynahs (genus *Acridotheres*) of India are mainly dull brown, with patches of naked yellow skin on the head and bold white flashes in the wing.

Feeding Most starlings are insect-eaters, although some forest-dwellers take fruits. The common starling and the Indian mynah *Acridotheres tristis* are omnivorous.

COMMON STARLING
Most songbirds molt twice a year, but the common starling has a single molt in late summer. The summer plumage (shown here) has a purple and green sheen.

Habitat Some species are arboreal birds of jungle and rain forest, but most inhabit open country, spending much of their time on the ground. Some, such as the common starling and the Indian mynah, live in close association with humans.

Well-known species Almost throughout the English-speaking world, the common starling is among the commonest of garden birds. Its plumage is black, glossed with green and purple, and spangled (in the nonbreeding season) with pale brown. Its song, an extraordinary jumble of squeaks, rattles, whistles and other apparently random sounds, is uttered freely from exposed perches on telephone wires or television aerials. It nests in an untidy jumble of grass and litter stuffed into any available cavity in a tree or a building, and it gathers in large noisy flocks to roost at night. The bird originated in Europe and owes its present more extensive distribution to deliberate introductions by humans.

FAMILY STURNIDAE
The family is native to the Old World, but the common starling has been widely introduced elsewhere.

SUPERB GLOSSY STARLING
A sight familiar to safari tourists in East Africa, the superb glossy starling *Spreo superbus* commonly visits campsites and picnic grounds.

MAGPIE-LARKS

The four Australasian species grouped in the family Grallinidae vary in many respects, but share one characteristic—they all build nests of mud on horizontal branches well off the ground. The species are the magpie-lark *Grallina cyanoleuca*, the torrent-lark *G. bruijni*, the white-winged chough *Corcorax melanorhamphus* and the apostlebird *Struthidea cinerea*.

Magpie-larks usually build their nest near water, and this individual has found a handy perch on which to sit out a flood.

Characteristics The magpie-lark and the torrent-lark are thrush-sized birds with glossy black-and-white plumage, and clear differences between the male and female. The white-winged chough is a sooty black bird with a curved bill. The apostlebird is gray with brownish wings and a black tail. These latter two species are very sociable and are usually encountered in family groups of five to twelve birds.

Reproduction Both parent magpie-larks build the nest, incubate the eggs, and brood and feed the nestlings. Pairs tend to stay

CLASSIFICATION

ORDER
PASSERIFORMES
FAMILY GRALLINIDAE
3 GENERA
4 SPECIES

FAMILY GRALLINIDAE
This small family is found in many habitats throughout most of Australia and New Guinea.

MAGPIE-LARK
This bird spends much of its time foraging on the ground for insects and their larvae, and also taking worms and mollusks. It has a loud *pee-wee* call, giving it an alternative common name.

together throughout the year in the same territory. Breeding is a cooperative affair for white-winged choughs and apostlebirds. Helpers share in nest-building, incubation, brooding and tending fledglings.

The torrent-lark's reproductive habits are not well known.

Habitat The magpie-lark is common throughout Australia and southern New Guinea in most habitats, while the torrent-lark inhabits the margins of fast-flowing streams in New Guinea's mountains. The other two species are confined to the shrublands and woodlands of eastern Australia.

BIRDS OF PARADISE

Birds of paradise (family Paradisaeidae) are well known for the males' ornate plumage and fantastic courtship displays. A tree full of these birds, all in simultaneous display quivering their long lacy flank plumes and calling hysterically, is one of the most spectacular sights among birds. Most species are confined to New Guinea.

SUPERB BIRD OF PARADISE
The male superb bird of paradise *Lophorina superba* has breast plumage that flares out to make "wings" during its solo display.

CLASSIFICATION

ORDER
PASSERIFORMES
FAMILY PARADISAEIDAE
17 GENERA
42 SPECIES

Characteristics Generally stout- or long-billed and strong-footed, they are crowlike in appearance and size. The males

of most species have spectacular plumage, some with long flank and tail plumes; females are generally drab.

Reproduction Males of the various polygynous species court females in differing ways, but the best known are the members of the genus *Paradisaea,* in which males congregate to display in mating grounds, known as leks. The males call from and hop about

lek perches and spread raised plumes while posturing and performing dances in unison. Studies of leks of the raggiana bird of paradise *P. raggiana* revealed that most visiting females mate with the same male, presumably the dominant and most fit on the

FAMILY PARADISAEIDAE
Birds of paradise are confined to the Australasian region, and are most abundant in New Guinea.

lek. In this way, females optimize the quality of male genes for their offspring. Nests are bulky cups of leaves, ferns, orchid stems and vine tendrils in a tree fork. The female lays one to three beautifully marked and colored eggs.

Habitat Birds of paradise forage for fruits in rain forest, moss forest or swamp forest, and may visit nearby gardens. Most of them live in mountainous areas of New Guinea and immediately adjacent islands. The exceptions are two species that inhabit the Moluccan islands, and four species that occur in parts of Australia.

BOWERBIRDS

Bowerbirds (family Ptilonorhynchidae) are noted for their sexual displays. But unlike birds of paradise, the emphasis is not on spectacular plumage, but on the often elaborate "bower" constructed by the male. There are four bower types: court, mat, maypole and avenue.

Court and mat Only the tooth-billed bowerbird *Scenopoeetes dentirostris* makes a "court," by clearing a patch of forest floor and decorating it with upturned fresh leaves. The only mat bower is that of the rare Archibold's bowerbird *Archboldia papuensis*, which accumulates a mat of fern fronds on the forest floor and decorates it with snail shells, beetle wing cases, fungus, charcoal and other items, and drapes orchid stems on the perches above.

Maypole and avenue Maypole bowers—stick structures built around one or several sapling

SPOTTED BOWERBIRD
A male spotted bowerbird *Chlamydera maculata* spends much of his time tending his bower of sticks decorated with white and pale green objects.

stems—are built by the four New Guinea gardener bowerbirds (genus *Amblyornis*) and the golden bowerbird *Prionodura newtoniana* of Australia. The remaining eight species make avenue bowers, vertical stick walls standing in the ground. Avenues may be built and decorated with great attention to detail—some are even adorned with paint made of fruit pulp.

The pay-off In the end, attention to detail pays off. Studies of the Australian satin bowerbird *Ptilonorhynchus violaceus* show that females visit three or four bowers, and show a tendency to mate with males whose bowers are solidly built and elaborately ornamented.

BOWERS
The satin bowerbird of eastern Australia (right) builds a typical avenue bower, while the gardener bowerbird *Amblyornis flavifrons* of New Guinea (below) constructs a maypole bower.

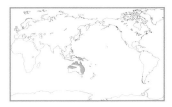

FAMILY PTILONORHYNCHIDAE
Nine species are peculiar to New Guinea, eight are found only in Australia, and two occur in both areas.

CROWS

Crows, rooks, ravens, jays, magpies and nutcrackers all belong to the family Corvidae. The majority are big, bold, conspicuous and versatile songbirds, and they appear in most habitats in most parts of the world. The harsh, unmusical call of many crow species is a familiar sound in rural areas the world over.

CLASSIFICATION

ORDER
PASSERIFORMES
FAMILY CORVIDAE
c. 25 GENERA
c. 117 SPECIES

ROOK
The rook is often seen foraging in fields and pastures in open cultivated country. An adult is shown here (in the foreground) with an immature bird.

Characteristics Most are medium to large in size, have nostrils covered with bristles, and relatively long legs with characteristic scaling. Color varies from the somber black of the raven through to the brilliant reds and greens of the Asian magpies.

Feeding They forage on the ground, probing with their strong bills to search for insects, tear meat from carcasses, harvest berries or pick up fallen seeds. Many of the smaller species forage in the forest canopy, and some specialize in harvesting particular foods such as nuts and pine seeds, which they may hide in caches to be relocated and used later.

Reproduction In many species, a breeding pair tends to reside in one area or territory with the same partner for as long as they both survive, and they defend that area

BLUE JAY
The blue jay *Cyanocitta cristata* is a common bird of parks and gardens from the North American Atlantic coast to the Great Plains.

against intrusion by others of the same species. Other species, such as the rook *Corvus frugilegus* and jackdaw *C. monedula*, prefer to nest colonially. Both parents build the nest and feed the young, but only the female incubates the eggs and broods the nestlings; during that time she is fed by the male.

Habitat Members of the family Corvidae are mainly found in forests, open woodland, scrubland and plains.

EURASIAN JAY
The Eurasian jay *Garrulus glandarius* is never found far from trees. It is known for its habit of burying acorns in summer and retrieving them in times of shortage in winter.

FAMILY CORVIDAE
The crow family is extremely widespread, occurring on all continents except Antarctica.

285

MAGPIE

The raucous call of the magpie *Pica pica* is a common sound in much of Europe, Asia and North America, from farmland and woods to urban areas. They are watchful birds and will give noisy alarm calls if cats or birds of prey are near. In areas where magpies are common, their bulky nests, used year after year, are conspicuous features of the landscape.

CLASSIFICATION

**ORDER
PASSERIFORMES**
FAMILY CORVIDAE
c. 25 GENERA
c. 117 SPECIES

Characteristics

From a distance magpies look black and white, but a closer view reveals green, purple and blue in the gloss of the black feathers. Males are slightly larger than females, and pairs are usually formed for life. Birds with short tails are lowest in rank. Magpies often form loose flocks of 20 birds outside the breeding season.

Like its fellow corvids, the magpie is gregarious, bold and inquisitive.

Feeding They are omnivores, and occasionally rob other birds' nests of eggs and young.

Reproduction Magpies build a bulky, domed structure of branches, lining the inside with fine branches and roots.

JACKDAW

The jackdaw *Corvus monedula* of Europe and Asia is one of the most social and intelligent of birds. It prefers to breed in colonies, doing so in parts of its range in towns and villages, often in or near church towers or in holes in old trees. Jackdaws are usually seen flying or foraging together as pairs.

The male jackdaw sometimes displays its gray nape during courtship by raising its crown feathers while pressing its bill against its breast.

Characteristics The jackdaw is about 13 inches (33 cm) in length. Except for the gray nape, its plumage is black. The sexes are alike. In winter, jackdaws flock together with other corvids, particularly rooks. Then they can be recognized by their smaller size and quicker movements.

Feeding Jackdaws are omnivores and feed in fields, farmland, parks and gardens.

Reproduction There is an elaborate courtship ceremony in which the male bows, with wings and tail spread. Jackdaw pairs stay together for life. The male and female build a bulky nest of branches lined with hairs and feathers in a hole or crevice in a tree, cliff or building. The female alone incubates the three to six eggs. The nestlings are fed by both parents.

CLASSIFICATION

**ORDER
PASSERIFORMES**
FAMILY CORVIDAE
c. 25 GENERA
c. 117 SPECIES

FINCHES
AND
SEED-EATING PASSERINES

The word "finch" is used to describe a number of different groups of seed-eating passerines. Typically, these birds are small, averaging about 6 inches (15 cm) in length, and have short, conical, attenuated bills reflecting their seed-eating habits. There are, of course, many exceptions to this general description, and the various finch families display a number of distinct differences in bill shapes, plumage patterns, habitat preferences and reproductive behavior. Yet overall the similarities are remarkable. The finches provide an excellent example of convergent evolution—of unrelated animals growing to look like one another because they have the same basic way of life.

EMBERIZINES

The Emberizidae, a large family of 560 species in 134 genera, can be broken down into several subfamilies. One of them, the Emberizinae, includes 279 species in 65 genera, which are thought to have originated in the New World and then dispersed to the Old World in several separate colonizations. The subfamily includes the sparrows and various finches of the New World, and the buntings of the Old World.

Characteristics These birds are approximately 6 inches (15 cm) in length, and all have the short, conical bills characteristic of finches. Most species of typical buntings of the genus *Emberiza* tend to have brown-streaked body plumage. The pointed crest and glossy blue-black plumage of the male crested bunting *Melophus lathami* and the dark-blue plumage of the Chinese blue bunting *Latoucheornis siemsseni* are unusual in the group. The sparrows are

YELLOWHAMMER
The Eurasian yellowhammer *Emberiza citrinella* is often first noticed by its song.

mostly brown and streaked, although many species are attractively colored—for example, the rufous and green of some towhees (genus *Pipilo*) and brush-finches (genus *Atlapetes*), and the bright orange-yellow of the saffron finches (genus *Sicalis*) of Central and South America.

Feeding Emberizines are generally seed-eaters, but often switch to a diet of insects when feeding their young. Birds in the grasslands of tropical Central and South America may clamp food

CLASSIFICATION

ORDER
PASSERIFORMES
FAMILY EMBERIZIDAE
SUBFAMILY
EMBERIZINAE
65 GENERA
279 SPECIES

RUFOUS-SIDED TOWHEE
The rufous-sided towhee *Pipilo erythropthalmus* has two distinct forms: the eastern (left) and the western (right).

items onto a perch with their feet and then pull off pieces with their bill.

Reproduction The majority of emberizines build a cup-shaped nest of grasses, roots and other plant fibers. Most tend to be monogamous or occasionally bigamous. Females of the white-crowned sparrow *Zonotrichia leucophrys* engage in "extramarital affairs" so that some 40 percent of their offspring are "illegitimate."

Habitat There are 42 species in the Old World and 234 in the New World. Emberizines occupy a variety of habitats, including grasslands, brushy areas, forest edges and marshes.

EMBERIZINAE
Species of emberizines can be found in all continents except Australia and Antarctica.

CARDINALINES

The subfamily Cardinalinae consists of 39 species in 9 genera, and is distributed throughout the Americas. Some, notably the "buntings" (genus *Passerina*), are very colorful. All cardinalines are thick-billed finches, and they differ from the more slender-billed emberizines, described earlier, in structure of palate, tongue and jaw musculature.

CLASSIFICATION

ORDER
PASSERIFORMES
FAMILY EMBERIZIDAE
SUBFAMILY
CARDINALINAE
9 GENERA
39 SPECIES

NORTHERN CARDINAL
A male northern cardinal *Cardinalis cardinalis* adds a splash of color to a holly bush in winter.

Characteristics The males of some species may have much brighter plumage than the females—for example, the cardinals (genus *Cardinalis*), the buntings (*Passerina*) and some of the grosbeaks (*Pheucticus*); but in the 12 *Saltator* species of Central America, the West Indies and South America, both sexes are similar in color, being mostly green and brown. Some species that breed in North America, such as the dickcissel *Spiza americana* and the indigo bunting *Passerina cyanea*, spend the winter in Central America; the latter has been the subject of fascinating studies on various aspects of migration, especially orientation using the stars and the Earth's magnetic field.

Feeding Cardinalines tend to be seed-peelers, removing the husks and swallowing the kernels whole. As well as seeds, fruits and insects are also eaten.

PAINTED BUNTING

The painted bunting *Passerina cris* breeds in thickets and weedy tangles across the southeastern United States; it winters in Central America.

Reproduction All cardinaline species build cup-shaped nests placed in trees or bushes. Males of the black-headed grosbeak *Pheucticus melanocephalus* and rose-breasted grosbeak *P. ludovicianus* assist the female in incubation and have the peculiar behavior of singing while sitting on the eggs. The cardinal *Cardinalis cardinalis* is well known for its regional song dialects.

Habitat These birds occupy a diversity of habitats in North, South and Central America.

Well-known species The handsome indigo bunting returns in April from its winter home in Mexico and Central America, to nest in the woodlands and overgrown fields of the east and south of the United States. The female is brown overall, paler below, with diffuse dusky streaking on her chest. After nesting, the male's bright blue is molted for an overall brown plumage punctuated with blue patches. The nest is a cup of grass and bark strips at low to mid levels in shrubs.

In the eastern United States, a flash of bright blue across a trail may indicate the presence of a male indigo bunting.

DARWIN'S FINCHES

The Galapagos finches may have been the starting point for Charles Darwin's theory of evolution. The differences in appearance of the finches on this remote archipelago led Darwin to the belief that species were not immutable, but can change over time—in other words, evolve.

Darwin's visit In 1835 the young Charles Darwin visited the Galapagos Islands in HMS *Beagle*. As he studied the local wildlife, he became intrigued by the finches, which varied in certain ways—especially in bill shape—from island to island. He theorized that these were all descendants of a single ancestral finch species which had reached the islands long ago. Over a long period, different species had arisen in response to the different conditions on each island.

A diversity of forms Some of the first finches to reach the islands continued to occupy seed-eating niches, so the larger islands have large-, medium- and small-billed species (*Geospiza magnirostris*, *G. fortis* and *G. fuliginosa*), which eat large, medium and small seeds respectively. One species evolved a longer bill and feeds on cactus flowers and fruits as well as seeds (*G. scandens*). Another evolutionary line led to the tree-dwelling finches, which feed on fruits, buds, seeds and insects.

Remarkable adaptations The woodpecker finch uses a twig or cactus spine to dislodge insects from beneath bark or from cracks in rotten wood. The warbler finch *Certhidea olivacea* adopted the way of life of a warbler and gleans small insects from foliage and twigs. Perhaps most remarkable of all, the ground or sharp-billed finch *Geospiza difficilis*, feeds on blood from seabirds. It perches on nesting boobies, pecks at the base of their wing and tail feathers, and laps up the blood that oozes out.

DARWIN'S FINCHES
Arising from a single ancestral species that probably looked very much like the bird in the center, Darwin's finches have evolved into a number of species that now occupy most islands and most habitats in the Galapagos Islands.

Sharp-billed or vampire finch—blood

Tree finch—insects

Warbler finch—insects

Woodpecker finch—insects
(extracted with cactus spine)

Ancestral seed-eating ground finch

Tree finch—plant material

Large cactus ground finch—cacti

Large ground finch—seeds

CARDUELINE FINCHES

The subfamily Carduelinae is part of a large family of finches, the Fringillidae, with a very widespread distribution. Apart from such well-known birds as greenfinches, goldfinches, siskins, crossbills and bullfinches, this group includes one of the most popular of all pets, the canary.

Characteristics These are small songbirds with conical bills. Many are brightly colored, and females are duller than males. Most Northern Hemisphere species are migratory, and many exhibit nomadic behavior. Although canaries are the most renowned cardueline singers, many other species produce beautiful songs. Domesticated canaries are descendants of the canary *Serinus canaria*, endemic to the Azores, Canary and Madeira Islands.

COMMON CROSSBILL
The common crossbill *Loxia curvirostra* uses its unusual bill to extract seeds from spruce cones.

Feeding Cardueline finches eat primarily seeds, buds and fruits. Insects do not make up a substantial proportion of the diet, even during the nesting season. This is distinctive, because most grain- and fruit-eating songbirds switch over to insects during

CLASSIFICATION

ORDER
PASSERIFORMES
FAMILY FRINGILLIDAE
SUBFAMILY
CARDUELINAE
16 GENERA
119 SPECIES

nesting. The carduelines, in contrast, feed their nestlings a mix of predigested plant material, including seeds and buds.

Reproduction They typically nest well off the ground in shrubs and trees, although a few species have developed close commensal relationships with humans (for example, the house finch *Carpodacus mexicanus* of North America) and may nest on buildings. An unusual aspect is that cardueline young defecate in the nest, so that the fecal material builds up on the walls and the rim; in other birds, the young either eject feces out of the nest or package fecal material in a sac that is removed by the adults.

Habitat Most species occur in subarctic, temperate or desert regions; the few that occur near the Equator inhabit mountainous regions with temperate climates. They do not breed natively in Madagascar, Australasia or the Indian subcontinent south of the Himalayas, although they have been introduced to many non-native regions.

SUBFAMILY CARDUELINAE
Carduelines are found in the Americas, Africa and Eurasia, with the greatest diversity in the Himalayan region.

GREENFINCH
The greenfinch *Carduelis chloris* is widespread in Eurasia, north Africa and Asia Minor. This pair is feeding on rose hips.

297

CHAFFINCHES

The chaffinches (subfamily Fringillinae) are the only fringillid finches that lack red or yellow in their plumage. There are three species: the brambling *Fringilla montifringilla*; the blue chaffinch *F. teydea*; and, one of the most widely known finches of European fields and gardens, the common chaffinch *F. coelebs*.

The male common chaffinch is brightly colored and handsomely patterned.

THE CHAFFINCH'S SONG

The common chaffinch played a prime role in birdsong research. It was the first species in which the interplay between song, innate vocal drives and learning was studied extensively. By playing recordings of songs at specific times during the growth of chaffinches, researchers found that a learning period early in life lasts about a year and is followed by a silent period. After that, the birds engage in a period of practice, during which their vocalizations crystallize into a song.

Characteristics

The common chaffinch and the brambling are mainly brown above. The males are boldly patterned; the females are duller. The males of the blue chaffinch are evenly colored blue.

Feeding All chaffinches feed on seeds, buds, fruits and insects.

CLASSIFICATION

ORDER
PASSERIFORMES
FAMILY FRINGILLIDAE
SUBFAMILY
FRINGILLINAE
1 GENUS
3 SPECIES

298

GROWING FAMILY
A female common chaffinch tends its young. The chicks will grow rapidly on a diet of nutritious caterpillars.

Habitat The common chaffinch and the brambling are primarily Eurasian, inhabiting open woods, gardens and farmlands; bramblings have a more northerly and westerly distribution than common chaffinches, breeding from Scandinavia to Siberia. The blue chaffinch is confined to the Canary Islands, where it inhabits mountain pine forests.

Reproduction The common chaffinch builds a cup-nest of grass and moss lined with hair and feathers in a tree or bush. The brambling builds a deep nest in a tree and lays six or seven eggs. The blue chaffinch places its nest in a pine or laurel tree, often at a great height.

Well-known species The common chaffinch is one of the most frequently seen birds in Europe in woodland, open country with trees, and parks and gardens. The bird's loud song of *pink-pink* carries a considerable distance; the main song uttered in flight consists of a soft *tyup*. In winter, these birds form large flocks, which feed on seeds on farmland or forage in gardens.

WAXBILLS

The waxbills (Estrildinae) form a subfamily of the family Estrildidae. These small birds are common in grassy areas of the Old World, mainly Africa. Their cheerful air, bobbing courtship displays and diet of seeds make them attractive as cage birds, so the behavior of many species is better known from watching them in captivity than in the field.

Characteristics Waxbill plumage is often highly colored, an example being the violet-eared waxbill *Chraeginthus granatinus*. A typical feature of the waxbills is the colorful markings inside the mouth of nestlings. In the red-billed firefinch *Lagonosticta senegala*, the juvenile mouth marking is bright orange-yellow with black spots on the palate and two shades of blue in the light-reflecting tubercles at the corners of the mouth. The bright gape guides the feeding behavior of the parent to the begging young. Other kinds of firefinches—and indeed, most other estrildids—each have their own particular mouth pattern. The patterns may be important to the parents in recognizing their young. The mouth colors of the young disappear when the birds are fully grown.

MELBA FINCH
During the dry season, the melba finch *Pytilia melba* uses its sharp bill to dig into termite nests.

CLASSIFICATION

ORDER
PASSERIFORMES
FAMILY ESTRILDIDAE
SUBFAMILY
ESTRILDINAE
16 GENERA
69 SPECIES

SUBFAMILY ESTRILDINAE

The waxbills inhabit Africa, southern Asia and Australasia, with most species found in sub-Saharan Africa.

Feeding Waxbills eat mainly grass seeds, but during the breeding season many also feed on termites.

Reproduction Waxbill pairs stay together in a close social bond, perch together in physical contact, preen each other, and rear their young together. One species is the small red-billed firefinch, which builds its nest of grass and the feathers of domestic or guinea

RED-BILLED FIRE FINCH

This is one of the most common of all African birds. In the villages where they often nest, they are known as "animated plums."

fowl. Adults usually live less than a year and maintain their populations by repeated breeding, rearing several broods in a season. They breed when rains produce a fresh crop of grass seeds.

Habitat These birds are familiar inhabitants of wooded grassland throughout much of Africa and in some parts of South-East Asia.

GRASSFINCHES

The grassfinches of the subfamily Poephilinae are part of the family Estrildidae. The group's best known species is the zebra finch *Taeniopygia guttata* (below), which is widespread in dry regions of Australia, where it feeds on grass seeds and insects. It is highly nomadic and breeds in loose colonies after rain. These birds are well adapted to their dry habitat: Their metabolic rate is lower than that of other finches (reducing the need for water), and they excrete less water than do other birds.

GOULDIAN FINCH

The parrot-finches (subfamily Erythrurinae) live in South-East Asia, northern Australia and on tropical islands of the western Pacific. They are distinguished by their beautifully colored and patterned plumage. One of the most colorful is the Gouldian finch *Erythrura gouldiae*, an inhabitant of grassland and open woodland in northern Australia.

CLASSIFICATION

ORDER
PASSERIFORMES
FAMILY ESTRILDIDAE
SUBFAMILY
ERYTHRURINAE
1 GENUS
12 SPECIES

Characteristics This bird is about 5½ inches (14 cm) long. There are three forms: The most common has a black face, but 20 to 30 percent of birds have a crimson face outlined with black, and a smaller proportion have a dull yellow face. Both sexes have identical coloring, but the female is duller. They are social birds, and live together in small flocks.

Feeding Gouldian finches feed on a range of grass seeds. When feeding, they prefer to cling to grass stems and pick out the seeds. They also eat insects, catching them in midair, and when breeding become almost wholly insectivorous.

Reproduction They nest in hollows in trees or termite mounds. Several pairs may nest close together.

GOULDIAN FINCH
This bird's bold coloring has made it a popular cage bird, which may be one reason why its numbers have declined in recent years.

MANNIKINS

Mannikins (subfamily Lonchurinae) are similar to waxbills, but have thicker bills and different courtship displays. One species has a close association with humans. Society finches are a domesticated strain of the white-rumped munia *Lonchura striata* developed centuries ago in China; they are used as foster parents for other estrildid finches in captivity.

Characteristics Mannikins lack the bright plumage coloration of other estrildid finches, being mainly of somber appearance, with browns, white and black, or gray featuring in their plumage.

Feeding Their diet consists mainly of seeds. The white-rumped munia *Lonchura striata* feeds in irrigated rice fields, eating the rice and the protein-rich green algae that grow there.

Reproduction In the courtship display, males characteristically ruffle the feathers of the head, breast and rump while singing. The breeding seasons of some white-rumped munias in Malaysia are determined by manmade cycles of rice cultivation. Nests are thatched with grass.

Habitat These finches typically favor rank grasslands, often near swamps, and in South-East Asia are often found in or near rice fields.

JAVA SPARROW
Native to South-East Asia, the Java sparrow *Padda oryzivora* is widely known as a popular cage bird.

CLASSIFICATION

ORDER
PASSERIFORMES
FAMILY ESTRILDIDAE
SUBFAMILY
LONCHURINAE
3 GENERA
37 SPECIES

WEAVERS

The weavers (family Ploceidae) are a largely African family of 126 species, with a few of those species in Asia and islands of the Indian Ocean. The family is subdivided into buffalo-weavers, sparrow-weavers, true weavers (which include bishops and widow finches), and whydahs. True weavers are dealt with here. Colonies of hundreds of these birds' nests are conspicuous in the African landscape.

RED BISHOP
The red bishop *Euplectes orix* inhabits reedbeds in Africa. Nonbreeding flocks of this gregarious species may comprise hundreds of birds.

Characteristics Most male true weavers have brightly colored plumage, although some species are black. Females are mainly brown. Sexual dimorphism in size and plumage is extreme among bishops and widow-birds. Bishops are named for the hood of red or yellow in the males' breeding plumage. Some long-tailed species are called "widows" (after the train or tail, as in a widow's mourning veil).

Feeding Some forest-dwelling weavers eat insects, but the majority of species feed on grass seeds, though they may feed

CLASSIFICATION

ORDER
PASSERIFORMES
FAMILY PLOCEIDAE
SUBFAMILY
PLOCEINAE
9 GENERA
c. 100 SPECIES

FAMILY PLOCEINAE
True weavers inhabit sub-Saharan Africa and southern Asia. The largest number of species is in Africa.

insects to their young. The red-billed quelea *Quelea quelea* is a locustlike scourge of cultivated grains in Africa.

Reproduction When making a nest, the male weaver first builds a swing to perch upon, then extends the swing into a ring, and adds a covered basket, keeping the ring as the entrance. He pushes and pulls the nest material into loops and knots around other blades of grass—a process similar to basket-weaving. Some species build a ball-like nest with an entrance hole in one side. Others finish the nest with a long entrance tube of woven grass. Females are attracted to the male as he hangs upside-down while clinging to the nest, waving his wings in flashes of yellow and black; the female inspects the nest, and if it is to her liking she lays and rears a brood by herself. Females prefer to nest with males in larger colonies.

Habitat Most of the 100 species live in grasslands or marshes.

MASKED WEAVER
This male masked weaver *Ploceus velatus* is putting the finishing touches to his intricately woven nest.

WHYDAHS

Whydahs are remarkable for two things: the very long tails of the males (used in courtship flights), and their practice of laying their eggs in the nest of a foster species. The foster parents incubate the eggs and rear the young whydahs along with their own brood. Young whydahs even have the same juvenile mouth markings and begging calls as the nestlings of their foster species.

PIN-TAILED WHYDAH
The male pin-tailed whydah *Vidua macroura* uses its long tail to attract females in impressive display flights.

Characteristics Outside the breeding season, male and female are about 6 inches (15 cm) long. But the male's breeding plumage includes immensely long tail feathers, greatly increasing his overall length. Males have mostly black or dark blue plumage, with white, yellow or reddish markings. In many species, the females look much like sparrows.

Reproduction Each whydah species is a brood parasite of a particular waxbill species.

For example, the straw-tailed whydah *Vidua fischeri* lays its eggs in the nests of the grenadier *Uraeginthus ianthinogaster.*

Habitat All species are found in Africa, mostly in savanna.

CLASSIFICATION

ORDER
PASSERIFORMES
FAMILY PLOCEIDAE
SUBFAMILY
VIDUINAE
1 GENUS
20 SPECIES

HOUSE SPARROW

Several of the 33 species of Old World sparrows (family Passeridae) have lived in close association with humans for centuries. The house sparrow *Passer domesticus* probably spread from the Middle East along with the movement of agriculture into Europe about 7,000 years ago; then, as Europeans colonized other parts of the world in the nineteenth century, it went with them.

CLASSIFICATION

ORDER
PASSERIFORMES
FAMILY PASSERIDAE
3 GENERA
33 SPECIES

Characteristics House sparrows are about 6 inches (15 cm) in length. The male is quite handsome, with chestnut-coloured head stripes and a black bib. In winter, his bill is a dusky palish brown, but in summer, it becomes blacker. Males with larger bibs are dominant over small-bibbed males. During fights among them, these bibs are shown off by pushing the chin and breast forward. The female and juvenile are brownish, and lack the bib.

Feeding They eat a variety of foods, including seeds, insects, bread and scraps.

Reproduction In courtship, several male sparrows surround the female, chirping loudly. The nest is a bulky dome of grass and straw placed in a cavity (such as beneath roof tiles) or in dense foliage. Two to six whitish eggs are laid.

FEATHER CARE
Routine feather care and maintenance is vital for birds. The house sparrow cleans up by "bathing" in dust.

CLASSIFICATION TABLE

The following list is based on *Check-list of Birds of the World* by J.L.Peters, E.Mayr, J.C.Greenway Jr., *et al.*, 1931–87, 16 volumes, Cambridge, Massachusetts, Museum of Comparative Zoology.

CLASS AVES

ORDER STRUTHIONIFORMES	**RATITES AND TINAMOUS**
Struthionidae	Ostrich
Tinamidae	Tinamous
Rheidae	Rheas
Casuariidae	Cassowaries
Dromaiidae	Emu
Apterygidae	Kiwis
ORDER PROCELLARIIFORMES	**ALBATROSSES AND PETRELS**
Diomedeidae	Albatrosses
Procellariidae	Shearwaters
Hydrobatidae	Storm petrels
Pelecanoididae	Diving petrels
ORDER SPHENISCIFORMES	**PENGUINS**
Spheniscidae	Penguins
ORDER GAVIIFORMES	**DIVERS**
Gaviidae	Divers (loons)
ORDER PODICIPEDIFORMES	**GREBES**
Podicipedidae	Grebes
ORDER PELECANIFORMES	**PELICANS AND THEIR ALLIES**
Phaethontidae	Tropicbirds
Pelecanidae	Pelicans
Phalacrocoracidae	Cormorants, anhingas
Sulidae	Gannets, boobies
Fregatidae	Frigatebirds

ORDER CICONIIFORMES — HERONS AND THEIR ALLIES

Ardeidae	Herons, bitterns
Scopidae	Hammerhead
Ciconiidae	Storks
Balaenicipitidae	Whale-headed stork
Threskiornithidae	Ibises, spoonbills
Cathartidae	New World vultures

ORDER PHOENICOPTERIFORMES — FLAMINGOS

Phoenicopteridae	Flamingos

ORDER FALCONIFORMES — RAPTORS

Accipitridae	Osprey, kites, hawks, eagles, Old World vultures, harriers, buzzards, harpies, buteonines
Sagittariidae	Secretarybird
Falconidae	Falcons, falconets, caracaras

ORDER ANSERIFORMES — WATERFOWL AND SCREAMERS

Anatidae	Geese, swans, ducks
Anhimidae	Screamers

ORDER GALLIFORMES — GAMEBIRDS

Megapodiidae	Megapodes (mound-builders)
Cracidae	Chachalacas, guans, curassows
Phasianidae	Turkeys, grouse, etc

ORDER OPISTHOCOMIFORMES — HOATZIN

Opisthocomidae	Hoatzin

ORDER GRUIFORMES — CRANES AND THEIR ALLIES

Mesitornithidae	Mesites
Turnicidae	Hemipode-quails (button quails)
Pedionomidae	Collared hemipode (plains wanderer)
Gruidae	Cranes
Aramidae	Limpkins
Psophiidae	Trumpeters
Rallidae	Rails
Heliornithidae	Finfoots
Rhynochetidae	Kagus
Eurypygidae	Sunbittern
Cariamidae	Seriemas
Otididae	Bustards

CLASSIFICATION TABLE continued

ORDER CHARADRIIFORMES — WADERS AND SHOREBIRDS

Family	Common name
Jacanidae	Jacanas
Rostratulidae	Painted snipe
Dromadidae	Crab plover
Haematopodidae	Oystercatchers
Ibidorhynchidae	Ibisbill
Recurvirostridae	Stilts, avocets
Burhinidae	Stone curlews (thick knees)
Glareolidae	Coursers, pratincoles
Charadriidae	Plovers, dotterels
Scolopacidae	Curlews, sandpipers, snipes
Thinocoridae	Seedsnipes
Chionididae	Sheathbills
Laridae	Gulls, terns, skimmers
Stercorariidae	Skuas, jaegers
Alcidae	Auks

ORDER COLUMBIFORMES — PIGEONS AND SANDGROUSE

Family	Common name
Pteroclididae	Sandgrouse
Columbidae	Pigeons, doves

ORDER PSITTACIFORMES — PARROTS

Family	Common name
Cacatuidae	Cockatoos
Psittacidae	Parrots

ORDER CUCULIFORMES — TURACOS AND CUCKOOS

Family	Common name
Musophagidae	Turacos, louries (plaintain-eaters)
Cuculidae	Cuckoos, etc

ORDER STRIGIFORMES — OWLS

Family	Common name
Tytonidae	Barn owls, bay owls
Strigidae	Hawk owls (true owls)

ORDER CAPRIMULGIFORMES

Steatornithidae
Podargidae
Nyctibiidae
Aegothelidae
Caprimulgidae

ORDER APODIFORMES

Apodidae
Hemiprocnidae
Trochilidae

FROGMOUTHS AND NIGHTJARS

Oilbird
Frogmouths
Potoos
Owlet nightjars
Nightjars

SWIFTS AND HUMMINGBIRDS

Swifts
Crested swifts
Hummingbirds

ORDER COLIIFORMES

Coliidae

ORDER TROGONIFORMES

Trogonidae

ORDER CORACIIFORMES

Alcedinidae
Todidae
Momotidae
Meropidae
Coraciidae
Upupidae
Phoeniculidae
Bucerotidae

ORDER PICIFORMES

Galbulidae
Bucconidae
Capitonidae
Ramphastidae
Indicatoridae
Picidae

MOUSEBIRDS

Mousebirds

TROGONS

Trogons

KINGFISHERS AND THEIR ALLIES

Kingfishers
Todies
Motmots
Bee-eaters
Rollers
Hoopoe
Wood-hoopoes
Hornbills

WOODPECKERS AND BARBETS

Jacamars
Puffbirds
Barbets
Toucans
Honeyguides
Woodpeckers

ORDER PASSERIFORMES

Suborder Eurylaimi	BROADBILLS AND PITTAS
Eurylaimidae	Broadbills
Philepittidae	Sunbirds, asitys
Pittidae	Pittas
Acanthisittidae	New Zealand wrens

Suborder Furnarii	OVENBIRDS AND THEIR ALLIES
Dendrocolaptidae	Woodcreepers
Furnariidae	Ovenbirds
Formicariidae	Antbirds
Rhinocryptidae	Tapaculos

Suborder Tyranni	TYRANT FLYCATCHERS AND THEIR ALLIES
Tyrannidae	Tyrant flycatchers
Pipridae	Manakins
Cotingidae	Cotingas
Oxyruncidae	Sharpbills
Phytotomidae	Plantcutters

Suborder Oscines	SONGBIRDS
Menuridae	Lyrebirds
Atrichornithidae	Scrub-birds
Alaudidae	Larks
Motacillidae	Wagtails, pipits
Hirundinidae	Swallows, martins
Campephagidae	Cuckoo-shrikes, etc
Pycnonotidae	Bulbuls
Irenidae	Leafbirds, ioras, bluebirds
Laniidae	Shrikes
Vangidae	Vangas
Bombycillidae	Waxwings
Hypocoliidae	Hypocolius
Ptilogonatidae	Silky flycatchers
Dulidae	Palmchat
Prunellidae	Accentors, hedge-sparrows
Mimidae	Mockingbirds, etc
Cinclidae	Dippers
Turdidae	Thrushes
Timaliidae	Babblers, etc
Troglodytidae	Wrens
Sylviidae	Old World warblers

Muscicapidae	Old World flycatchers
Maluridae	Fairy-wrens, etc
Acanthizidae	Australian warblers, etc
Ephthianuridae	Australian chats
Orthonychidae	Logrunners, etc
Rhipiduridae	Fantails
Monarchidae	Monarch flycatchers
Petroicidae	Australasian robins
Pachycephalidae	Whistlers, etc
Aegithalidae	Long-tailed tits
Remizidae	Penduline tits
Paridae	True tits, chickadees, titmice
Sittidae	Nuthatches, sitellas, wallcreeper
Certhiidae	Holarctic treecreepers
Rhabdornithidae	Philippine treecreepers
Climacteridae	Australasian treecreepers
Dicaeidae	Flowerpeckers, pardalotes
Nectariniidae	Sunbirds
Zosteropidae	White-eyes
Meliphagidae	Honeyeaters
Vireonidae	Vireos
Emberizidae	Buntings, tanagers
Parulidae	New World wood warblers
Icteridae	Icterids (American blackbirds)

Fringillidae	Finches
Drepanididae	Hawaiian honeycreepers
Estrildidae	Estrildid finches
Ploceidae	Weavers
Passeridae	Old World sparrows
Sturnidae	Starlings, mynahs
Oriolidae	Orioles, figbirds
Dicruridae	Drongos
Callaeidae	New Zealand wattlebirds
Grallinidae	Magpie-larks
Artamidae	Wood swallows
Cracticidae	Bell magpies
Ptilonorhynchidae	Bowerbirds
Paradisaeidae	Birds of paradise
Corvidae	Crows, jays

313

INDEX

Entries in *italics* indicate illustrations and photos.

ACKNOWLEDGMENTS

Weldon Owen would like to thank the following people: Sarah Anderson, Lisa Boehm, Trudie Craig, Janine Flew, Peta Gorman, Michael Hann, Aliza Pinczewski, Puddingburn Publishing Services (index)

TEXT Luis F. Baptista, Arnoud van den Berg, Anthony H. Bledsoe, Walter E. Boles, Peter L. Britton, P. A. Clancey, Charles T. Collins, Francis H. J. Crome, John P. Croxall, S. J. J. F. Davies, Jon Fjeldså, Clifford B. Frith, Stephen Garnett, Colin J. O. Harrison, Tom van der Have, Steve Howell, Guido Keijl, Alan Kemp, Scott M. Lanyon, Terence Lindsey, Kim W. Lowe, S. Marchant, H. Elliott McClure, Dominic Mitchell, Penny Olsen, Kenneth C. Parkes, Robert B. Payne, Michael R. W. Rands, Ian Rowley, E. A. Schreiber, Lester L. Short, G. T. Smith, Rich Stallcup, Frank S. Todd

ILLUSTRATIONS Mike Atkinson/The Garden Studio, Alistar Barnard, Jocelyne Best, Anne Bowman, Stephanie Cannon, Gerald Driessen, Mike Gorman, Frits Jan Maas, David Kirshner, Frank Knight, Stan Lamond, Jeff Lang, Karel Mauer, Robert Mancini, Robert Morton, Maurice Pledger, Tony Pyrzakowski, Sue Rawkins, Trevor Ruth, Trevor Weekes, David Wood, Weldon Owen Archives

PHOTOGRAPHS Ad-Libitum/Stuart Bowey; Auscape: J. Cancalosi, Ferrero-Labat, M. P. Kahl, Tui De Roy; Bruce Coleman Collection: M. P. L. Fogden, Hans Reinhard; Corel Corporation; Oxford Scientific Films: Tui De Roy, Tony Tilford; Steve Turner; Survival Anglia/Alan Root; The Australian Museum/C. Bento

CONSULTANT EDITOR Joseph Forshaw is a Research Associate in the Department of Ornithology at the Australian Museum and a Corresponding Fellow of the American Ornithologists' Union